THE
SNOWBALL
EFFECT

USING DIVIDEND & INTEREST REINVESTMENT
TO HELP YOU RETIRE ON TIME

TIMOTHY MCINTOSH

Published by Eckerd Press Co. San Antonio, Texas.

This is a work of non-fiction

Published simultaneously in Canada

For general information on our other products and services or for technical support, please contact our Customer Care Department within the United States at 877-762-2974, outside the United States at 317-572-3993 or fax 317- 572-4002.

Eckerd Press Co. also publishes its books in a variety of electronic formats. Some content that appears in print may not be available in electronic formats. For more information about Eckerd Press products, visit our web site at www.eckerdpressco.com.

Library of Congress Cataloging-in-Publication Data:

McIntosh, Timothy J.

The Snowball Effect; A Winning Investment Strategy of Using Dividend & Interest Reinvestment to Help You Retire on Time

Includes bibliographic references and index

ISBN-10: 0-692-75530-6

ISBN-13: 978-0-692-75530-3

1. Portfolio Management 2. Investments 3. Dividends

Printed in the United States of America
10 9 8 7 6 5 4 3 2 1

ABOUT THE AUTHOR

Timothy J. McIntosh serves as portfolio manager at SIPCO. He oversees aspects of major client accounts and serves as the lead portfolio manager for the firm's large cap value and corporate bond portfolios.

Mr. McIntosh holds a Bachelor of Science Degree in Economics from Florida State University. He has also attained a Master of Business Administration (MBA) degree from the University of Sarasota and a Master of Public Health Degree (MPH) from the University of South Florida. He is a Certified Financial Planner (CFP). Mr. McIntosh is the author of *The Bear Market Survival Guide*, *The Sector Strategist*, and the *Comprehensive Financial Planning Strategies for Doctors*. He has been featured in the *Wall Street Journal*, *New York Times*, *USA Today*, *Investment Advisor*, *Fortune*, *San Antonio Express News*, and *The Tampa Bay Times*. Mr. McIntosh served as an adjunct finance professor at Eckerd College from 1998 to 2008. He and his wife, Kim, have two sons and reside in Tampa, Florida.

CONTENTS

PRAISE FOR THE SNOWBALL EFFECT

"In his new book, "The Snowball Effect", author Timothy J. McIntosh says that "time is the best ally of the long-term, buy and hold income investor." He goes on to show that patient investors will benefit enormously from the long-term compounding that dividend paying stocks provide investors. He makes the case that investors should ignore the short-term and focus on the compounding benefits that only long-term investors can enjoy. A simple, yet very effective strategy. I highly recommend his book to all long-term investors."

**~James P. O'Shaughnessy, author of
"What Works on Wall Street"**

"Dividends and their reinvestment are friends of the value investor - put the two together and you can witness the wonders of compounding. Mr. McIntosh illustrates how such a strategy can snowball and lead to large sums of wealth for the patient investor."

-Mebane Faber is a co-founder and the Chief Investment Officer of Cambria Investment Management. Mr. Faber has authored numerous white papers and many books including "The Ivy Portfolio" and "Global Value".

If you spend any time watching the stock market, you probably get caught up in its daily gyrations. Stocks are up! Stocks are down! It's a bull market! No, it's a bear market! Of course, that's the wrong thing to do. Timothy McIntosh's book, The Snowball Effect, reminds you that you have an ally in the stock market: Dividends, which you can collect in good markets and bad. This book, drawn from McIntosh's years of experience as an investment manager and student of the market, will show you how to make money in stocks in good times and bad.

— **John Waggoner, senior columnist, *Investment News***

"Excellent information for long-term investors. Mr. McIntosh makes a compelling case for tapping into sources of yield to produce superior total returns, and he thoroughly demonstrates how dividend-paying stocks and selling covered calls contribute to such a strategy."

-John Dobosz is deputy editor of investing content for Forbes and the editor of the *Forbes Dividend Investor*.

Timothy McIntosh's new book, "The Snowball Effect," is a valuable contribution to the body of work focused on dividend investing. I found Chapter 3 ("The Promise of Reinvested Income") especially relevant and powerful.

-Chuck Carlson, CFA, is Chief Executive Officer of Horizon Investment Services LLC and the author of nine books, including "*The Little Book of Big Dividends*"

INTRODUCTION

"I never attempt to make money on the stock market. I buy on the assumption that they could close the market the next day and not reopen it for five years."

— *Warren Buffett–*

ANY INVESTOR MIGHT believe that stocks have always traded since the opening of the New York Stock Exchange (NYSE) in 1792. But there have been notable times when all trading was halted. The most pre-eminent period was right before World War I when the NYSE shut its trading system down on July 31st, 1914. The primary impetus was the closure of the Vienna stock exchange three days earlier after Austria-Hungary declared war on Serbia. The leaders of the NYSE were forced to follow as stock prices plunged across Europe the next day. The exchange would not re-open until December 15th, a period of 136 days. This period ended up being the longest interlude in NYSE history of no trading. Although investors who were counting on capital appreciation from their stocks were disappointed, those who owned dividend-bearing stocks kept receiving their dividend checks without interruption during those tumultuous times.

The investors who didn't have to worry during these times were focused on collecting income from their investments instead of relying on capital appreciation to raise their net worth. This isn't critical only when the stock market is closed—in fact, it's critical because more often than not, and repeatedly for very long stretches of time, stock market appreciation is anemic. For example, in January 1966, the Dow Jones Industrial Average (Dow) reached 995. For the next *seventeen years* the Dow would remain stagnant. The Dow would not surpass the 995 price level without looking back until December 1982.

What Is the Dow?

The Dow Jones Industrial Average (Dow) is an index of thirty blue-chip US stocks. Still going strong after 117 years, it is the oldest continuously running US market index. It is called an *average* because it was originally computed by adding up all of the prices of its stocks and dividing by the total number of stocks in the index. (It's very first average price of industrial stocks, recorded on May 26, 1896, was 40.94.) The methodology remains the same today, but the divisor has been changed to preserve historical continuity.

The Dow is the best-known market indicator in the world, partly because it's old enough that many generations of investors have become accustomed to quoting it, and partly because the US stock market is the largest in the world. The Dow began with only twelve components in 1896 and rose to twenty in 1916. The thirty-stock average made its debut in 1928, and the number has remained constant ever since.

This book is not written for stock speculators, but for those investors that can embrace the concept of becoming an income investor. An income investor—one who embraces a buy-and-hold state of mind and who buys dividend-bearing stocks and bonds—has an innate mental advantage over the average investor. An income investor realizes that no matter what the stock market might do, she will continue to reap the rewards of dividends and interest from her investments. She knows she should only invest in corporate entities that pay her a portion of its income from profits or interest from the loan she is providing. In this manner, she can rest assured that her future goals will ultimately be met through the process of compounding interest and dividends.

> Snowball ([snoh-bawl); verb (used without object): to grow or become larger, greater, more intense, etc., at an accelerating rate.

The title of this book is *The Snowball Effect*, with good cause. In reality, time is the best ally of the long-term, buy-and-hold income investor. The initial results are slow to come about and not that impressive, but in due time, compounding dividends and interest end up *snowballing* into mindboggling returns, even during periods of market stagnation.

The first use of the word *snowball* as a noun came about circa 1400, in Germany. It was referred to in West Frisian as *sniebal*, in Middle Dutch as *sneubal*, and in German as *Schneeball*. The image of a snowball increasing in size as it rolls along had been used since at least 1613, and the first printed use of the term as a verb meaning *to increase rapidly* occurred in 1929, in the *Denver Post*.

"Every man who is buying and selling on margin is gambling. And the snowball they have been rolling uphill got too big and heavy and rolled back over them."

— *Denver Post*, October 29, 1929

How ironic, then, that the term *snowball* was used as a verb on the occasion of the great market crash of 1929—and that it was used in the context of the stock market. I've titled this book *The Snowball Effect* as an illustration of my theory that building up dividends and interest over time is <u>*the single most critical step*</u> in building wealth.

I start in Chapter 1, with an introduction to the four largest secular (secular is an adjective used to describe a long-term time frame, usually at least 10 years) bear markets that have occurred since 1906. The long years between 1966 and 1982 are one of the most famous instances of long-term sideways or secular bear markets. The Dow also made no progress whatsoever from 1906 to 1924, 1929 to 1954, and, more recently, 2000 to 2011. Surprisingly common and long-lived, sideways markets go against the common wisdom published in most investment books: that "stocks always go up" and are a solid investment in the long term.

In Chapters 2 and 3, you'll find my analysis of the history of dividends and how higher-income stocks can be powerful ingredients in a recipe for investment success. Chapter 4 places the focus on small-cap stocks. I review the historical data and returns of small-cap stocks in comparison to large-cap companies and examine the dividend characteristics of small-cap firms. I also delve into micro-cap firms, the smallest within the investment universe. In Chapter 5, you'll learn all about bonds. I will concentrate much of the chapter on how corporate bonds are unique investment vehicles for an income investor. Chapter 6 examines the covered-call strategy, which can help you collect additional income from your stock portfolio by selling covered calls.

Last, in Chapter 7, I provide a guide to the future of investment returns and also a case study of a portfolio that puts my recommended screening process for stocks to work. There, I reveal how that portfolio would perform if we had another secular bear market from 2016 to 2025. I also list the top 100 dividend-bearing stocks (I call them the Top 100 Snowball Investments) for income investors—the type of stocks that allow you to reap high relative income and earn consistent returns, no matter what market malaise might transpire.

CHAPTER 1

THE TREACHEROUS SECULAR BEARS

"All the heroes of tomorrow are the heretics of today."

—Edgar Yipsel "Yip" Harburg, Lyricist, 1896–1981

LYRICIST YIP HARBURG (more about him in a bit) wrote these words in a poem about a quite different topic, the Hollywood blacklist of the 1940s and '50s. But Harburg's words were prescient about the financial markets as well. As mentioned in the introduction, secular stock market cycles are extended periods of time when markets deliver below- or above-average returns. Secular markets are tenacious: Sometimes lasting as long as one or two decades. Most importantly, they are *the* significant marker of investor performance over any extended period of time.

There are two types of secular markets; bear and bull. A bear secular market occurs when the market trend is sideways and the Dow doesn't climb above its previous high price level. My definition of a secular bear market might be poles apart than other analysts. I consider a secular bear market only to be over after the stock market crosses back above its previous high price and *never returns* below that price.

A secular bull market is an up trending market that continually sets new price highs until it reaches its price zenith. Now while it is accurate that stocks go up, overall, they do so in an incredibly inconsistent manner. This is because the market whipsaws through secular bear and bull markets over time. This leads me to address what is, in my opinion, the most misleading adage about the stock market: "the market always goes up."

Any student of history—and reality— could tell you that this simply is not true. As the table indicates below, the stock market can go through extended periods of time hallmarked by little to no price appreciation in stocks. These are branded secular bear markets. Table 1.1 maps the four long-term secular bear markets experienced over a 110-year span, from 1906 to 2015.

Start	End	Months	Years	Annualized Price Return
02/1906	06/1924	220	18	-0.24%
09/1929	11/1954	302	25	0.11%
02/1966	11/1982	200	18	0.21%
02/2000	11/2011	141	11	0.32%

Table 1.1: Long-Term Secular Bear Market Periods from 1906 to 2015

So now you know the truth—during the periods 1906–1924, 1929–1954, 1966–1982, and 2000–2011, almost 70 percent of the 110-year range, stock prices as measured by the Dow barely budged. That makes the common promise you'll hear from investment professionals of a 9 percent return from stocks over your investment lifetime both misleading and *wrong*.

Imagine an investor who began saving for retirement the year he turned thirty. While investment advisors are right to say investors should start saving young, like the fellow in this scenario, be glad you didn't turn thirty in 1966. That year ranks among the worst to begin long-term investments in stocks. Over the next eighteen years, our investor would have seen less than 1 percent growth in the value of his stocks on a price basis, but would be within ten years of retirement age.

Clearly, these facts go against the conventional wisdom investors have been told over the last thirty years. And the average investor, unfortunately, believes the hype. For each of the last five years, Natixis Global Asset Management has surveyed 7,000 individual investors around the world to understand their views on investment returns. In the 2015 survey, as in every previous year, participants were asked what average annual return they would need to achieve their financial goals. Their response? A return of 9.7 percent above inflation, almost a full point higher than the 9 percent reported in the 2014 survey. Even more amazing, 72 percent of the investors Natixis spoke to said that they believed these expectations of returns were realistic.

It's not just individual investors that have pie-in-the-sky expectations. The California Public Employees' Retirement System (CalPERS) also maintains the charade, assuming future annual investment returns of 7.5 percent to 8 percent. CalPERS actuaries, who compile and analyze statistics and use them to calculate risks, returns, and premiums, have gone on record urging board members to lower the annual investment assumption to well below 7.5 percent. You read that right—according to CalPERS' *own experts*, the odds of reaching the intended target are unlikely (in fact, they've set the likelihood at well below 50 percent). Not surprisingly, experts in the field acknowledge that investment return predictions over any investment horizon are extremely unreliable, at best.

What most investors are unaware of is the fact that time and time again, constructive investment returns for stocks have come in short-term time spurts. A great example—the six years from

March 2009 to March 2015, during which the Dow rose by a remarkable 159 percent and logged more than 2,000 days without posting a major decline. Just like that, investors saw the value of their stock holdings more than double. But the 2009-2015 period also demonstrated once again the unequal distribution of investment returns. Many pundits are now arguing we have moved from a secular bear market (2000-2011) to a secular bull market. This may be the case. A secular bull, or upward-trending, market occurs when each successive high point is higher than the previous one. But secular bull markets are actually more rare and almost always shorter than secular bear markets (Table 1.2)

Start	End	Months	Years	Annualized Price Return
07/1924	08/1929	63	5	29.14%
12/1954	01/1966	135	11	8.63%
11/1982	01/2000	206	17	14.97%

Table 1.2: Long-Term Secular Bull Market Periods from 1906 to 2015

Secular bull market cycles generally begin after capital markets have been soft, providing muted annualized investment returns over a long period of time. One methodology to predict when a secular bear or bull market will occur is through an analysis of the P/E ratio of the stock market.

A price-earnings (P/E) ratio values a company by measuring its current share price relative to its per-share earnings. A conventional P/E ratio compares a company's share price to either the past year's earnings or forecast earnings, typically for the next twelve months. For example, suppose that XYZ company is trading at $60 per share and its earnings over the last twelve months came in at $4 per share. The P/E ratio for XYZ would be calculated as 60/4 or 15. This has been the average P/E ratio for all stocks since 1910. But stocks do not always trade at a level of 15 times earnings.

At the start of a secular bull market, the P/E ratio for all stocks is generally quite low, typically under 10. In the long run, stock returns tend to reflect earnings growth. But during the three secular bull markets shown in Table 1.2 above, stocks advanced much faster than earnings. This is known as the P/E multiple expansion effect.

In the long-lived bull market that prevailed from 1982 to 2000, stock prices grew *much* faster than earnings. The P/E multiple on the Dow nearly tripled, accounting for 45 percent of the stock market's total return. Earnings growth during this period held at 6.5 percent for firms indexed by the Dow, but the average return for the Dow was 15.1 percent per year. The Dow's starting P/E ratio was 8 in 1982; by the end of 1999, it had reached 30. The three big secular bull markets of the twentieth century returned, on average, just over 15 percent per year for the stocks in the Dow.

Why the Dow?

The Dow Jones Industrial Average, aka the Dow, is the second oldest stock index in the United States (preceded only by the Dow Jones Transportation Average). Named after former *Wall Street Journal* editor Charles Dow and statistician Edward Jones (no relation to the Edward Jones who founded his own eponymous investment firm), the Dow has been a key measure for large US-based blue-chip stock prices since its inception on May 26, 1896. I've used the Dow as the touchstone in this book because the data is so far-ranging (going back to 1906) and because the index itself is a fair representation of all large-cap US stocks. In addition, the companies represented in the Dow have maintained a high level of dividends, or cash payments to shareholders.

> I chose not to use the more popular Standard & Poor (S&P) 500 index, as its history goes back only to 1923 and began as an index of only a few stocks. It did not grow to its current size of 500 members until 1957. Additionally, not all S&P 500 stocks pay dividends, but all Dow stocks do.

You may think that the remarkable progress of stocks during the 1982-2000 period was due to superior earnings growth. Remarkably, during the secular bear market of 1966 to 1982, earnings for the companies in the Dow grew by 7 percent per year—surpassing their earnings growth during the bull market of 1982-2000. The big difference; starting P/E ratios. Because the Dow's P/E ratio was 18.5 in 1966 and not 8, as it was in 1982, returns for investors remained solidly anemic over those ensuing eighteen years.

That doesn't mean that stocks can't continue higher from a particular P/E level. There is no set ceiling for a stock market to reach. For example, the P/E ratio continued higher in the late 1990s, ultimately reaching 30 by the top of the Internet stock bubble. That was much higher than the 18.5 reached in 1966. But after 2000, investors faced severe overvaluation and the potential for an extreme retrenchment in stocks. The extreme high P/E values of 2000 were a giant red flag indicating danger to come as investors crossed into the new century. From 2000 to 2002 and again from 2008 to 2009, the Dow fell by more than 40 percent in value, and it didn't surpass its previous price peak again until 2011.

Of course, investors can't pick and choose the timing of their investments or know when P/E levels might top out. If the crest level of the market occurs within an investor's peak earning years (forty to sixty years of age) or after retirement (beyond the age of sixty), bear market cycles can be devastating. If an investor was fortunate enough to start the bulk of her wealth building in 1982, one of the greatest bull markets in history likely carried her portfolio to supreme heights until the end of the century. But the reverse became true in 2000, where the stock market topped out and remained below the index's previous high for the next eleven years. Developing and maintaining strategies to survive secular bear markets is the most important consideration any prudent investor can have. Let's examine the four major bear markets of the last 110 years.

THE SECULAR BEAR MARKET OF 1906 TO 1924

On January 19, 1906, the Dow topped out at a price level 103. Then the stock index fell off a cliff, losing 48.5 percent of its value over the next twenty-two months. With that, the first secular bear market cycle of the twentieth century began.

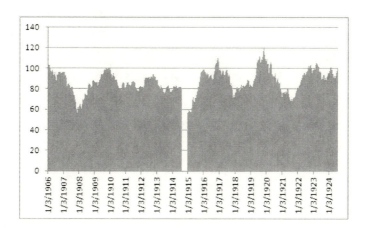

Figure 1.1: Dow Price Chart from 1906 to 1924

The collapse of the stock market over this period was caused by several factors—first among which was the infamous San Francisco earthquake of 1906. Up to that point, an economic boom had been raging since the start of the century. But the earthquake caused immediate economic repercussions, as bank deposits were unavailable for weeks on the West Coast. A run on US currency began not just in California, but also throughout the rest of the country.

The run on dollars continued throughout the year and into 1907; then, a crescendo of events in New York pushed the entire banking system into a crisis known as the Panic of 1907. In October of that year, copper-miner-turned-banker F. Augustus Heinze and his stockbroker brothers Otto and Arthur tried to manipulate the markets to benefit Augustus's firm, the United Copper Company. When their plot failed, the price of the stock collapsed. Investors rushed to pull their money out of the disgraced company, and an already tenuous banking system became unglued.

Heinze's primary bank in Montana failed, which then caused the linked Knickerbocker Trust Bank of New York to collapse. The breakdown of the Knickerbocker touched off an avalanche of withdrawals across the banking sector. At the height of the crisis, on November 2, 1907, financier J.P. Morgan gathered nearly 50 New York bankers in his library. He pledged large sums of his own money to fix the panic and convinced his fellow bankers to do the same.

With Morgan's intervention, a deeper banking crisis was averted. The Dow ultimately bottomed two weeks later at a price of 53. Immediately after the Panic, Congress enacted the Aldrich–Vreeland Act, a piece of legislation that addressed some of the financial system's most pressing needs. It only went so far, however, and put off the day of reckoning about the bigger question: What sort of federal bank could work in a country with a long history of rejecting central banks?

Instead, members of Congress formed the Fed's precursor, the National Monetary Commission. The legislators traveled to the great capitals of Europe to learn about how their banking systems worked and apply what they learned to the Commission, but it was ultimately ineffective. The Federal Reserve System would not be complete for another eight years.

Year	High/Low	Year	High/Low
1/19/1906	103	5/13/1918	82.16
4/26/1906	92.44	11/3/1919	119.62
11/15/1907	53	12/22/1919	103.55
4/24/1908	70.01	1/3/1920	109.88
11/19/1909	100.53	1/14/1920	102
10/10/1910	81.91	2/3/1920	99.96
9/25/1911	72.94	8/24/1921	63.9
9/30/1912	94.15	12/15/1921	81.5
1/14/1913	84.96	1/10/1922	78.59
12/24/1914	53.17	10/14/1922	103.43
4/9/1915	65.02	11/27/1924	92.03
11/21/1916	110.15	3/20/1923	105.38
8/28/1917	86.12	10/27/1923	85.76
12/19/1917	65.95	11/3/1924	103.89

Table 1.3: Secular Bear Dow Highs and Lows from 1906 to 1924

After hitting its November 1907 lows, the Dow nearly doubled over the next two years. By November 19, 1909, it had climbed over the 100 mark. But the rally was short-lived.

As time went on, the economy slowed, and by July 1910, the Dow had dipped by more than 20 percent. The economy officially slipped back into recession in the third and fourth quarters of 1910, and the economic system was further plagued by crop failures and droughts during 1911. In the same year, the central plains scorched through a heat wave that extended from March to September. Another recession hit the US economy in 1913, and in July 1914, the stock market closed for four months as World War I began.

The Dow Changes

On October 4, 1916, the Dow changed its makeup. National Lead, Peoples Gas, General Motors, and US Steel were dropped, and twelve new companies joined the list. Following is the full list of its twenty industrial stocks in 1916:

American Beet Sugar, American Can, American Car & Foundry, American Locomotive, American Smelting, American Sugar, American Telephone & Telegraph (AT&T), Anaconda Copper, Baldwin Locomotive, Central Leather, General Electric, Goodrich Republic, Iron & Steel, Studebaker, Texas Company, US Rubber, US Steel, Utah Copper, Westinghouse, Western Union

After it reopened on December 14, 1914, the Dow collapsed. Just a little more than two months later, on February 24, 1915, it had fallen by more than 30 percent, back down to 54.

The early 1915 collapse was largely caused by the escalation of the Great War. Germany began bombing the city of London in early January, 1915. The carnage continued, as on May 7 of that same year—less than a year after World War I had erupted across Europe—a German U-boat torpedoed and sank the RMS Lusitania, a British ocean liner en route from New York to Liverpool, England. More than 1,100 of the 1,900 passengers and crew members on board perished, including more than 120 Americans. But after the sinking of the Lusitania, the Dow began a slow ascent that continued through the summer. The index ultimately reached a high of 99.21 on December 27.

In the next year, 1916, the Dow continued higher, reaching 110.44 that November. But as Germany continued sinking ships from neutral countries into early 1917, its relations with the

United States soured. After April 6, 1917, the date the United States declared war on Germany, the Dow fluctuated in a range from 75 to 110 until November 3, 1919, when it reached a new high of 118.92—a high that would not be surpassed for the next five years. That same day, Peter J. Maloney paid $100,000 for a seat on the New York Stock Exchange (NYSE), breaking a record for the highest price paid that had stood since 1906.

By the conclusion of World War I, those in charge of the US economy found themselves in a miserable state. The skyrocketing debt load caused by the war touched off a new recession in early 1920. Annual consumer price inflation rates had risen above 20 percent and federal spending had been slashed, from $18.5 billion in 1919 to $6.4 billion. The relatively young Federal Reserve System also raised interest rates during the period in an effort to slow inflation. These tactics worked, as deflation became rampant and prices fell by more than 15 percent over the next 18 months.

In 1921, the unemployment rate peaked at nearly 12 percent, but afterward, deflation abated and the economy slowly came out of recession. Just two short years later, the economy was booming and the unemployment rate had dropped to less than 3 percent. In July 1924, the Dow bobbed over the 100 mark and finally on November 3, 1924 it had crossed over the 103 mark set in 1906 for the last time. The decade known as the Roaring Twenties had arrived, and the markets entered a new phase. During the next several years until the top in 1929, the Dow would advance nearly 300 percent, closing at 381 on September 3, 1929.

The Secular Bear Market of 1929 to 1954

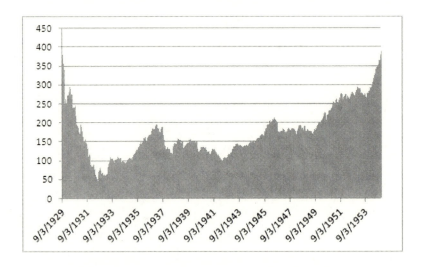

Figure 1.2: Dow Price Chart from 1929 to 1953

October 29, 1929 will be forever known as Black Tuesday. As the panic escalated, investors traded some 16 million shares on the NYSE in a single day. Billions of dollars in wealth were lost, and thousands of investors were wiped out.

The Dow had begun its decline on October 18, 1929. Panic set in, and on October 24, a then-record 12 million shares were traded. Investment companies and leading bankers responded quickly, trying to soothe the markets by buying up large blocks of stock.

But nothing could stop the events of Black Tuesday, and stock prices completely collapsed. In the aftermath, the US economy sank into the Great Depression. Prices continued to drop, and by 1932 stocks were worth a fraction of the value they held in the summer of 1929. The boom of the Roaring Twenties had turned to bust.

Written in 1930 by lyricist Edgar Yipsel "Yip" Harburg and composer Jay Gorney, "Brother, Can You Spare a Dime?" is perhaps the best known song of the 1930s. The situation faced by the song's protagonist hit home for a lot of Americans, as it dramatized the betrayal many of them felt. Having built a nation and an economy they truly believed in, many Americans felt that Wall Street and the political establishment had conspired to destroy it all. By 1933, nearly half of America's banks had failed, and nearly 15 million citizens were unemployed.

A reprieve came with reforms instituted by the incoming US President, Franklin D. Roosevelt. Roosevelt's New Deal mitigated some of the nastiest elements of the Great Depression, but on July 8, 1932, the Dow plummeted to its lowest Depression-era point, closing at 41.22. By that day, it had tumbled nearly 90 percent from its peak in 1929.

Starting in July 1932, the Dow began to slowly climb, but economic conditions showed little improvement. One year later, on July 18, 1933, the Dow reached 108.97—amazingly, still below its value in November 1916. For the next two years, the Dow remained in a tight range from 85 to 110.

Despite continued economic problems, in 1935, the Dow again began to rise, reaching a high of 184 by November 1936. During this time, the American Midwest was gripped by a terrible drought that precipitated the Dust Bowl (also known as the Dirty Thirties). After years of improper management, the soil of the plains was vulnerable. As the earth became drier and drier during the drought, the relentless winds of the prairies whipped the topsoil away and plunged the people of the central United States into a dust cloud. With their land no longer arable, farmers had nothing to grow and nothing to sell. The drought and the Dust Bowl conditions came in three primary waves, 1934, 1936, and 1939–1940.

The Dust Bowl deeply affected the overall US economy; soon, the Recession of 1937–1938 began. By the spring of 1937, production, profits, and wages had been restored to 1929 levels, but unemployment remained high—only slightly below 25 percent. The US economy took a pointed downturn in the middle of 1937, touching off the recession. It lasted just over a year, through most of 1938.

At the time, most pundits blamed the recession on the Roosevelt administration. In 1937, Roosevelt decided to remove monetary stimulus in order to curb runaway inflation and reduce the deficit. The Dow was hit hard. Having reached 194 on March 10, 1937, the Dow then plunged by nearly 50 percent, reaching a low of 98.95 on March 31, 1938.

On September 1, 1939, German soldiers rumbled into Poland, and World War II had begun. The United States immediately declared its neutrality, but Wall Street investors were excited by the prospects of providing war materials overseas: The magazine *The Nation* ran an article entitled "Boom Is On." The Dow quickly rallied, reaching a level of 155.92 on September 12, 1939.

But by March 1942, as the United States became mired in war, the Dow had dropped below 100. Investor passion had flagged so much that even an average dividend yield over 9 percent wasn't enough to entice them. A seat on the NYSE sold for a mere $17,000 in 1942—versus $625,000 in 1929, or $100,000 as far back as 1906. Times had certainly changed on Wall Street.

The Dow would not cross its September 1939 high of 155 again until January 11, 1945. The index continued higher after the war, as the global economic recovery began in earnest. By January 1950, the Dow crossed over 200 and continued its upward trajectory, finally reaching 384 in November 1954. With that, the longest-running secular bear market in US history was finally over.

Year	High/Low	Year	High/Low
9/3/1929	383.85	4/28/1942	92.92
7/8/1932	41.22	2/1/1943	125.86
9/7/1932	79.93	7/24/1944	145.77

2/27/1932	50.16	7/22/1946	195.22
5/24/1933	84.29	3/16/1948	165.39
3/10/1937	194.4	8/18/1949	182.02
3/31/1938	98.95	11/26/1951	257.43
9/12/1939	155.92	1/5/1953	293.79
6/10/1940	111.84	1/19/1954	288.27
11/9/1940	138.12	7/13/1954	340.04
5/1/1941	115.3	11/24/1954	384.63

Table 1.4: Secular Bear Dow Highs and Lows from 1929 to 1954

THE SECULAR BEAR MARKET OF 1966 TO 1982

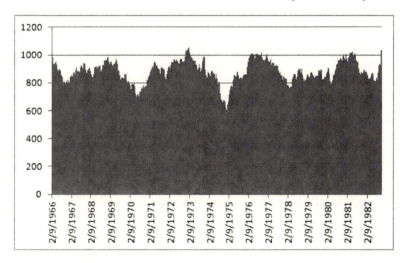

Figure 1.3: Dow Price Chart from 1966 to 1982

On February 9, 1966, the Dow reached 995.15—within striking distance of 1,000. From then until the end of 1982, both the US economy and markets were battered by a combination of rising interest rates and commodity prices. The Dow would flirt with 1,000 again and again throughout the period, but it would always fall back into a rigid range somewhere between 500 and 1,000. The mood among investors who followed a buy-and-hold strategy over the course of this long-lasting secular bear market can be summarized in a single word—irritated. The index spent the eighteen years following that dazzling peak in February 1966 in a series of political and economic quandaries.

First, the credit crunch of 1966 soured the markets. In early 1966, the US economy was entering its sixth year of relentless expansion, high economic growth, and low inflation. The unemployment rate was very low, only 4 percent. But during the first eight months of 1966, business and government sectors placed weighty demands for funds on the money and capital markets. US corporations had raised an astonishing $13 billion in new cash from the sale of stock securities—an increase of 25 percent over 1965.

To slow this growth and the resulting precipitous rise in new capital, Federal Reserve Bank (Fed) policies became much more restrictive over the summer of 1966 via open market operations and reserve requirement policy. This period, which became known as the Fed Credit Crunch, is recognized as the first noteworthy post-World War II financial crisis, namely because it was the first important intervention by the Fed since the war. The Dow fell by 22 percent, reaching 744 in October of that year. It climbed back to the mid-900s by 1967, only to falter once again due to worldwide concerns over the Vietnam War.

The index spent the next two years fluctuating in a narrow trading range. Rising inflation, increased deficits caused by defense spending, and monetary tightening sent the Dow into a dive by the start of 1969. An ensuing economic recession put an additional damper on investors' confidence, and the markets endured a vicious losing stretch, falling nearly by a third in 18 months. The market continued rattling around until student anti-war protesters were killed at Ohio's Kent State University in May 1970. The Dow was pummeled, falling by 7 percent over a two-week period.

In late 1972, the Dow scratched its way back up, reaching 1,036 on December 11. But the euphoria of crossing back over 1,000 was short-lived. A new bubble developed around the so-called Nifty Fifty stocks, which were hailed as the 50 best buy-and-hold large-cap stocks available. This bubble led to one of the biggest market drops of the century.

Economic and political turmoil ruled the day. In the next year, the Organization of the Petroleum Exporting Countries (OPEC) quintupled the price of oil; the reverberations of the move mired the United States in a deep recession. Between January 1973 and December 1974, the stock market's value plunged 45.1 percent. The largest part of its decline—17.6 percent over a three-week period—came in August 1974, in light of US President Richard Nixon's resignation. Unemployment rose steadily throughout 1974, ultimately reaching an apex of 8.7 percent, the highest rate since 1941, in March 1975. The prime lending rate among large US banks rose to a monstrous 15.7 percent.

Ultimately, 1975 turned out to be a solid year for stocks. As the Vietnam War finally drew to a close, the Dow embarked on a two-year advance of nearly 60 percent. But the market recovery was only temporary.

During the late 1970s, the United States was gripped by recession and soaring interest rates. The Dow stalled in 1977 and made no progress for the rest of the Carter administration—primarily because of pervasive stagflation, an economic condition that combines three negative factors: high inflation, high unemployment, and stagnant demand.

Economist Paul Volcker was appointed chairman of the Federal Reserve by President Carter in August 1979. Volcker took office ready to fight inflation and the other maladies facing the US economy, and Wall Street responded positively. Ronald Reagan's victory in the November 1980 election and the simultaneous economic recovery spurred a sizable market rally. Two weeks after the Republican landslide, the Dow crossed the 1,000 mark for the first time since the end of 1976. It then ascended higher, to 1,024, in the wake of a March 1981 failed assassination attempt on Reagan.

Year	High/Low	Year	High/Low
2/9/1966	995.15	10/4/1974	584.56
10/7/1966	744.32	9/21/1976	1,014.79
9/25/1967	943.08	2/28/1978	742.72
12/3/1968	985.21	9/11/1978	907.74
1/26/1970	768.88	4/21/1980	759.13
5/26/1970	631.16	4/27/1981	1,024.05
4/28/1971	950.82	8/12/1982	776.92
1/11/1973	1,051.7	11/14/1982	996.87

Table 1.5: Secular Bear Dow Highs and Lows from 1966 to 1982

Nonetheless, the US economy entered a recession in July 1981, and by September, the Dow had plummeted to 824. That fall, the Fed began slashing interest rates to stem the recession, but the action had little effect on the market. Continued high unemployment and economic stagnation conspired to send the Dow below 800 in the spring of 1982. Its descent persisted for the next five months.

In June 1982, a *Business Week* article titled "Running Scared from Stocks" captured the mood beautifully, and its timing was impeccable. Two months later, the Dow hit 776—rock bottom of the long secular bear market that had started back in February 1966.

Another interest rate cut and some positive economic news lit a fire under the Dow. In the latter half of August, it skyrocketed by 16 percent and crossed 900. By November 14, it surpassed 996 for the final time. A secular bull market was born, and the rest of the Reagan years would be known for exceptional stock market gains.

The amazing statistic from this long period of stagnation is how long it took for P/E ratio contraction. From 1966 to the end of the brutal 1973–1974 market downturn, the Dow went from trading at 22 times earnings to 14 times earnings. The next two temporary peaks in the market during the late 1970s ended at 11.8 and 9.1 times earnings, respectively. It was only after the last downturn in 1981/82 that the selling in the Dow would finally be complete. The Dow finally bottomed at a paltry P/E ratio of 8.

The Secular Bear Market of 2000 to 2011

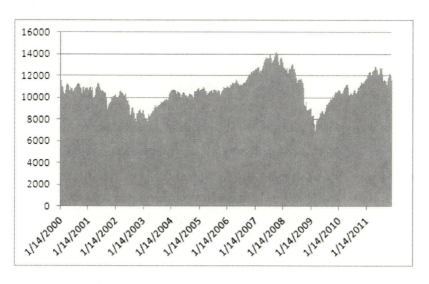

Figure 1.4: Dow Price Chart from 2000 to 2011

On January 14, 2000, the Dow reached a new high, 11,722. Just nine years earlier, on January 9, 1991, it had bottomed at 2,470.30. The Dow's fourfold increase was driven by a perfect balance of high economic growth, low inflation, and technological revolution—excess that hadn't been seen since the 1920s.

But the Dow's increase had a dark side: It had taken the index to nosebleed valuations as measured by P/E ratio. In January 2000, the P/E of the Dow was an astounding 32, twice the historical average.

From 1997 to 2000, the infamous Dot-Com Bubble was mostly to blame. This historic speculative market bubble was spawned by the founding of (and endless market curiosity about) countless new Internet-based companies commonly referred to as dot-coms.

Companies quickly discovered they could cause their stock prices to rise, or access huge influxes of venture capital, by simply adding an "e-" prefix or a ".com" suffix to their names. The technology company-laden National Association of Securities Dealers Automated Quotations System (NASDAQ) index climaxed at 5,132 on March 10, 2000—a mere two months after the Dow had reached its apex. Just as a rising tide lifts all boats, the steady climb of the NASDAQ and other dot-com companies led all stocks higher; even old-line firms like Pfizer and Coca-Cola traded at P/E ratios in the 40s. And the amalgam of rapidly increasing stock prices and easy venture capital funding led many investors to throw money at a plethora of inherently unprofitable firms.

Ultimately, fewer than half the dot-com companies that bloomed in the late 1990s survived the downturn that followed—many that were founded in 2000 went bankrupt within a year of going public. Bubble-fueled accounting scandals rocked the capital markets, and monolithic firms like Enron and WorldCom went bankrupt.

After the terrorist attacks of September 11, 2001, the recession that gripped the US economy deepened. The Dow fell to a low on September 21, 2001 of 8,235.81. A minor rebound off the lows was short-lived, and by 2002 the Dow had continued its slide. The market bottomed on October 9, 2002, when the Dow closed at 7,285.27.

Year	High/Low	Year	High/Low
1/14/2000	11,722.98	11/21/2007	12,799.04
9/21/2001	8,235.81	3/10/2008	11,740.15
10/26/2001	9,545.17	5/2/2008	13,058.2
3/19/2002	10,635.25	8/11/2008	11,782.35

10/9/2002	7,286.27	11/20/2008	7,552.29
1/6/2003	8,773.57	1/2/2009	9,034.69
8/16/2003	12,845.78	3/9/2009	6,547.05
10/25/2004	9,749.99	4/26/2010	11,205.03
11/3/2005	10,522.59	7/2/2010	9,686.48
12/27/2006	12,510.57	9/27/2010	10,812.04
10/9/2007	14,164.53	3/17/2011	11,774.54

Table 1.6: Secular Bear Dow Highs and Lows from 2000 to 2011

A rally that started in March 2003 continued for the next four years, as growth resumed after the Internet bust. Housing prices and consumer debt soared. During that period, the Dow nearly doubled, reaching a peak of 14,164.53 on October 9, 2007. Yet it stagnated for most of the next six months, reaching 13,058.20 on May 2, 2008.

In the days and months that followed, the housing market collapsed, the price of oil (and along with it, the price of food and other commodities dependent on transport) rose to dizzying heights. The Great Recession had begun, and the Dow would not surpass its 2007 levels until 2013. The ensuing stock market collapse was one of the greatest since the 1930s.

The Great Recession had many sources, starting with consumer debt and the housing bubble. Throughout the early 2000s, consumer debt grew at a shocking rate, hitting $2 trillion by 2004. As prices spiraled up, prospective homeowners feared being priced out of the market and took on risky mortgages. (Banks were only too happy to oblige them.) During the run-up in housing prices, the mortgage-backed securities (MBS) market and the credit default swaps (CDSs) became fashionable yet lethal financial products. As it was subject to virtually no regulation, the CDS market fell apart. The American dream of homeownership became a nightmare for thousands as they began to default on their mortgages. By December 2007, the United States economy was in a recession.

In March 2008, the huge Wall Street investment banking firm Bear Stearns was slammed with huge losses from the many MBS and CDS products it had underwritten; it ultimately failed. On September 7, 2008, with the Dow holding at 11,510.88, the Federal National Mortgage Association (Fannie Mae) and its sibling, the Federal Home Loan Mortgage Corporation (Freddie Mac) were taken over by the US government.

One week later, on September 14, 2008, the investment firm Lehman Brothers announced its collapse—the biggest bankruptcy filing in US history. The next day, markets plummeted and the Dow closed down 499 points, at 10,917. On September 19, 2008, US Treasury Secretary Henry Paulson proposed the Troubled Asset Relief Program (TARP), a bailout for financial institutions that involved making as much as $1 trillion in government funds available to acquire the institutions' poisonous debt and, hopefully, evade a total financial meltdown. The respite TARP provided was short; the economy continued its dive and the unemployment rate skyrocketed. By late October 2008, the Dow had fallen to 8,175.

Ultimately, the Dow lost 54 percent of its value over a seventeen-month period. Its low point came on March 6, 2009—6,443.28. As the government's efforts to patch the economy through stimulus began to take hold, the Dow began to rise consistently, finally breaking through 11,700 in March 2011. It would not cross its 2007 price high (14,164) until nearly two years later.

Consider Table 1.7, The Dow's Best and Worst Days in History. Better than any discourse, it shows in brief just how perilous the market can be. On its best day, the Dow shot up more than 15 percent, but on its worst, it plummeted by almost 23 percent.

The Best of Times			
Date	**Dow Closing**	**% Up**	**Context**
March 15, 1933	62.1	15.34%	The largest ever percentage gain in Dow history was posted in the depths of The Great Depression.
October 6, 1931	99.34	14.87%	President Hoover offered plans to revive the Depression-era business climate.
October 30, 1929	258.47	12.34%	Stocks recovered a few days after the great 1929 market crash, buoyed by buying activity by one investor, John D. Rockefeller.
September 21, 1932	75.16	11.36%	Indications of an economic recovery were helped by railroad freight activity.
October 12, 2008	9387.61	11.08%	Central bank actions led to optimism that the worst of credit crisis was over and the Treasury's TARP plan was outlined.
October 28, 2008	9065.12	10.88%	Investors expected the Fed to lower rates in response to the credit crisis.
October 21, 1987	2027.85	10.15%	Markets recovered lost ground after the 1987 crash.
August 2, 1932	58.22	9.52%	Hopes of a GM dividend and rumors that the Federal Farm Board has eased wheat surpluses pushed the market higher.
February 11, 1932	78.6	9.47%	Traders rejoiced over a Congressional bill that would ease financing through the Fed's discount window.
November 14, 1929	217.28	9.36%	The 1929 market experienced a classic "dead cat bounce" following a drop in share prices over the preceding weeks.

The Worst of Times			
Date	**Dow Closing**	**% Down**	**Context**
October 19, 1987	1738.74	-22.61%	Black Monday 1987: Stocks around the world crashed due to economic and geographic concerns.
October 28, 1929	260.64	-12.82%	Black Monday 1929: Speculation that had driven the market up in preceding years evaporated.

October 29, 1929	230.07	-11.73%	Black Tuesday 1929: Selling from the previous days continued to drive the market lower.
November 6, 1929	232.13	-9.92%	Share prices continued to suffer the effects of the historic crash days earlier.
August 12, 1932	63.11	-8.40%	Sellers driven by margin calls—who sold into a lack of liquidity—helped drive shares lower.
March 14, 1907	76.23	-8.29%	The Knickerbocker Crisis yielded panic selling, economic recession, and bank runs—and the market was hammered.
October 26, 1987	1793.93	-8.04%	Investors remained anxious following the Black Monday crash that occurred one week earlier.
October 15, 2008	8577.91	-7.87%	Recession fears, a gloomy Fed outlook, and weak retail sales drive stocks deeply lower.
July 21, 1933	88.71	-7.84%	Markets reacted to negative news regarding grain futures.
October 27, 1997	7161.14	-7.26%	A selloff in Asia continued into US markets as the triggering of market circuit breakers led to a shortened trading session.

Table 1.7: The Dow's Best and Worst Days in History

WHAT DOES IT ALL MEAN?

It's noteworthy that almost all the cumulative capital appreciation return the Dow has experienced in the past 110 years came about during three secular periods: 1924–1929, 1954–1966, and 1982–2000. The balance of the positive secular bull time period has been since 2011, when the Dow broke through the high level reached in 2000. In the intervening years, markets merely treaded water while the economy and earnings grew. This phenomenon continued until valuations (as measured by P/E ratios) eventually reached a trough at the lower end of that range, thus allowing a new secular bull market to arrive.

Secular bull markets thus have only prevailed for 39 years during the period from 1906 to 2015, but the majority of the period were years of price stagnation. In a secular bull market cycle, buying and holding stocks is the optimal strategy. As long as the secular bull market persists, stock appreciation accounts for the majority of stock gains. But when a secular bear market cycle begins, on the other hand, a simplistic buy-and-hold strategy could leave an individual's portfolio with roughly the same amount of money decades later. It also means that after inflation is taken into account, our investor actually loses money.

Obviously, it's in an investor's best interest to figure out when secular bear markets are likely to occur. This is not an easy assignment. But we know that in most cases, secular bear markets start after the markets have advanced much faster than earnings and P/E ratios reach nosebleed levels. To allow for a more elongated view of P/E ratios over time, one key statistic an investor can investigate is CAPE. Nobel laureate and economist Robert Shiller developed the cyclically adjusted price/earnings ratio (also known as CAPE) statistical process, and it can be a great indicator of when the troubles are likely to occur. CAPE is based on a market gauge originally used for individual stocks by Benjamin Graham and David Dodd, who intended to measure the price of a company's stock relative to average earnings over a ten-year period. Shiller customized it to adjust for inflation, with an aim to level out the economic and profit cycles and offer clearer perspective into a company's value than the traditional P/E ratio, which measures only a single year's profits. Examining earnings over a 10-year period smoothes out the picture and helps investors determine whether the market is undervalued or overvalued. The CAPE ratio has been demonstrated to have a high correlation with future investment returns from stocks.

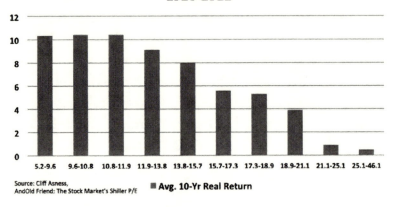

Avg. 10-Yr Real Return based on starting CAPE, 1926-2012

Source: Cliff Asness,
AndOld Friend: The Stock Market's Shiller P/E ■ Avg. 10-Yr Real Return

*Figure 1.5: Average 10-Year Real Return Based
on Starting CAPE, 1926 to 2012*

As this CAPE chart indicates in figure 1.5, when the average CAPE P/E is low at any given point in time, future ten-year investment returns are high. Conversely, when the stock market is priced at a high CAPE P/E ratio, future ten-year returns are virtually nonexistent.

An investor who attempts to build wealth during periods of high starting CAPE P/E ratios are almost always doomed to low future returns—at least from a long-term perspective. High stock market valuations, as measured by CAPE, drive low long-term future returns. Imagine that you are an investor who has set goals for retirement that will require a 9 percent annual return—the same that the 2015 Natixis survey participants felt was a reasonable ask. If secular bear years are more common than secular bulls, how will you reach those goals over an extended period of time? This is an extremely critical question, especially in 2016. As CAPE P/E levels have now returned to higher-than-average levels, due to the strong run-up in stocks since 2009, investors must develop a plan of action to survive the next secular bear market.

CHAPTER 2

THE POWER OF DIVIDENDS

"Do you know the only thing that gives me pleasure? It's to see my dividends coming in."

—John D. Rockefeller, 1896–1981

THE PREVIOUS CHAPTER made one fact very clear, and it's something every investor needs to be aware of. Secular bear stock markets are not rare; they are commonplace. The odds are extremely high that an investor will witness a secular bear market over his or her investment lifetime.

Thus, if you are only invested in stocks that offer the promise of significant capital appreciation gains (think Facebook and Tesla), you'd better hope that you're an outstanding stock selector. A safer bet: Focus on companies that pay dividends. Why? Dividend-paying stocks can insulate an investor from secular bear market cycles by providing income while stock prices stagnate.

Remember Table 1.1, which demonstrated that stocks had virtually no price return over the four extended secular bear markets? Consider Table 2.1, which examines the annualized returns of the Dow over the same periods with dividends taken into consideration. Although the returns still don't approach the overall 9.39

percent average return Dow stocks have yielded since 1906, they're noticeably positive. The conclusion: The only reliable way to make positive returns during secular bear market periods is to invest in dividend-paying stocks like those in the Dow.

Start	End	Annualized Return	Annualized Return with Dividends Reinvested
2/1906	6/1924	-0.24%	6.19%
9/1929	11/1954	0.11%	5.53%
2/1966	10/1982	0.71%	4.82%
2/2000	11/2011	0.32%	2.78%

Table 2.1: Secular Bear Market Annualized Returns with and without Dividends Reinvested

In fact, dividends have accounted for a substantial part—40 percent—of total investor returns over the last 110 years—not just during secular bear markets. In some decades that coincided with secular bear markets (1910–1920, 1930–1940, 2000–2010), dividends accounted for *more than 100 percent* of the total return from stocks, as shown in Table 2.2.

Decade	Dow Price Percentage Change	Dow Price Percentage Change with Dividends	Dividends Percentage of Total Return
1910s	-2.91%	44.8%	>100%
1920s	381.6%	422.4%	21.3%
1930s	-41.9%	14.1%	>100%
1940s	34.8%	135.0%	74.3%
1950s	256.7%	436.7%	41.2%
1960s	53.7%	107.9%	50.2%
1970s	17.2%	76.4%	77.4%
1980s	227.4%	370.5%	38.6%
1990s	315.7%	432.8%	27.0%
2000s	-24.1%	-9.1%	>100%

Table 2.2: Dividend Contribution of Dow Return by Decade
Source: Dow Jones

The Facts of Dividends

Companies pay portions of their profits to shareholders through the payment of dividends. A dividend is a payment made to eligible shareholders on a quarterly, semiannual, or annual basis. Most US companies that pay dividends do so quarterly, while non-US companies generally pay semiannual or annual dividends. Most companies try to maintain or increase dividends to keep shareholders happy and avoid negative publicity.

Dividends are normally quoted on a per-share basis, meaning that the dividend each shareholder receives is based on the number of shares that he or she owns. For example, if you own one hundred shares of stock in Company X and it decides to pay an annual dividend of $5 per share, your dividend would be $500 (100 shares × $5 per share). Sometimes, dividends are quoted in terms of a percentage of the current market price for a company's shares; for example, if Company Y announces a 2.5 percent dividend on its $100 share price, its shareholders will receive $2.50 per share owned. If you hold one hundred shares of Company Y, you'll receive a payment of $250.

Key Terms Every Dividend Investor Must Know

Cash Dividends: Cash payments made to stockholders paid on a per-share basis. Cash dividends are quoted either as a dollar amount or as a percentage of a stock's current market value and are typically paid out of the company's current earnings or accumulated profits. They are the most common type of dividend.

Date of Record: The date the company uses to determine which of its shareholders, or "holders of record,"

---

will receive a dividend distribution; all shareholders who own the stock two business days before that date (the ex-dividend date) receive dividends.

Ex-Dividend Date: Two business days before the date of record. If you purchase a stock on the ex-dividend date or afterward, you will not receive the next dividend payment. Instead, the seller receives the dividend.

Declaration Date: The date a company's board of directors announces that a dividend distribution will be forthcoming.

Dividend Coverage Ratio: The ratio between a company's earnings and its net dividend to shareholders. The dividend coverage ratio helps investors measure if a company's earnings are sufficient to cover its dividend obligations. For example, in 2016, Pepsi's dividend coverage ratio is expected to be 65 percent, as it will pay a dividend per share of \$3.01 against earnings expectations of \$4.73 per share. (\$3.01 ÷ \$4.73) = 65%.

Why Do Companies Pay Dividends?

Theory 1: The Bird in the Hand

Economists Myron Gordon[1] and John Lintner developed the infamous bird-in-the-hand theory, which proposes that investors prefer dividends to capital gains. The theory's name comes from the maxim "A bird in the hand is worth two in the bush." According to

---

[1] M.J. Gordon, "Dividends, Earnings, and Stock Prices," *Review of Economics and Statistics,* 41 (1959): 99–105.

the theory, capital gains are considered to be quite risky, and thus investors expect to be compensated by higher returns. The bird-in-the-hand, thus, is the dividend, and the bush is the capital gains.

To Gordon and Lintner, this places undue pressure on a corporation's leadership to deliver higher growth in the future. The theory suggests that dividends are the most relevant consideration of investing in a company; I find this to be an exceedingly compelling argument, particularly given the fact that during long periods of stock-market stagnation (i.e., 1966 through 1982), capital appreciation from equities is nonexistent.

Theory 2: Dividend Irrelevance

In counterpoint, economists Franco Modigliani and Merton Miller proposed the dividend irrelevance theory, which states a company's dividend policy has no impact on its cost of capital or on shareholder wealth. They pioneered the idea that dividends and capital gains are comparable when an investor considers returns on investment.

According to dividend irrelevance theory, the only consideration that affects a company's valuation is its earnings, which are a direct result of the company's investment policy and the future prospects. Much like their work on the capital-structure irrelevance proposition, Modigliani and Miller also theorized that if you are not taking into consideration taxes or bankruptcy costs, dividend policy is also irrelevant.

For example, assume that a company's dividend is excessive beyond expectations. An investor who receives the dividend could then use it to buy more stock. Likewise, if a company's dividend is smaller than he or she expected, an investor could sell some of the company's stock to replicate the expected cash flow.

Thus, according to Modigliani and Miller, dividends should be irrelevant to investors, as investors care little about a company's dividend policy since they can simulate their own. This theory also suggests that dividends are irrelevant by the arbitrage argument. By this reasoning, dividend distribution to shareholders is offset by external financing. Once dividends are distributed, the price of the stock decreases, thus nullifying any gains to investors.

Dividend irrelevance also implies that the cost of debt is equal to the cost of equity, as the cost of capital is not affected by leverage. Perfect capital markets do not exist, as taxes are always a factor. According to this theory, there is no difference between internal and external financing. But this hypothesis is false if flotation costs of new issues are taken into consideration.

Lastly, dividend irrelevance theory suggests that shareholder wealth is unaffected by dividends. But consider the transaction costs associated with the selling of shares to make cash inflows. That alone can lead investors to prefer dividends; an assumption of no uncertainty is simply unrealistic. Although dividend irrelevance theory is conceptually sound, I believe that it ignores the powerful effect dividend payments can have for investors during secular bear markets.

THEORY 3: TAX PREFERENCE

Taxes are important considerations for investors. Remember, capital gains are taxed at a lower rate than dividends. Thus, some theorize, investors may prefer capital gains to dividends. This is known as the tax preference theory. Of course, capital gains are not paid until an investment is sold. Investors can control when capital gains are realized, but they can't control dividend payments.

Capital gains are also not realized at the time of an investor's death. For example, consider an investor who purchased 1,000 shares in a company 50 years ago at a price of $2.00 per share. That price would be considered the cost basis of the stock. If the investor chose to sell his stake in the company in the present day and the shares were trading at $100 per share, he would have to pay taxes on capital gains of $98 per share, the difference between the cost basis and the present trading price. But if the investor dies and the shares transfer to his heirs through his estate, the cost basis is adjusted—or in tax parlance, "stepped up"—to the price of the stock at the time of the investor's death. In such an event, the heirs will not pay capital gains taxes on the stock's appreciation.

THE DIVIDEND PUZZLE

The pioneering works of Gordon (1959) and Lintner (1956, 1962) and Miller and Modigliani (1961) spurred an ongoing debate on dividend policy, which remains a controversial issue to this day. In a 1976 article, economist Fischer Black found no convincing explanation for why firms pay cash dividends; he titled the article "The Dividend Puzzle."[2] The dividend puzzle is a concept in finance in which companies that pay dividends are rewarded by investors with higher valuations, despite the fact that, according to many economists, investors shouldn't care whether a firm pays dividends.

According to this rationale, from the investor's point of view, dividends should have no effect on the process of valuing equity because investors already own (a piece of) the company. Therefore, the investor should be indifferent to receiving the dividends as cash or reinvesting them into more shares of the company. At the time Black wrote his paper, there was a wide gap between the tax rates on ordinary income (meaning dividends) and capital gains. The puzzle—why would corporations force investors to pay high ordinary tax rates on dividends when lower capital gains tax rates could apply to the sale of stocks?

---

2 Fischer Black, "The Dividend Puzzle," *Journal of Portfolio Management*, 2 (1976): 5–8.

Economist G.M. Frankfurter gave the puzzle a second look many years later, in a 1999 article that summarized[3] the previous literature. Like Black, Frankfurter concluded the puzzle still existed, despite changes to the tax code. He opined, "Investors love dividends."

Since 1999, many academics have followed on the writings of Black and Frankfurter. They've produced extensive and sometimes conflicting research, offering many alternative theories as to why firms pay dividends, or why they shouldn't, or even why the decision to pay dividends may be irrelevant. But to date, empirical evidence has yet to clearly support any of the theories set forth.

The Dividend Payment Process

Suppose Pepsi is planning to pay a dividend to its shareholders. Here's how the process will unfold.

- On January 28, Pepsi declares it will pay its regular dividend of $2.40 per share to holders of record on February 27, with payment to be received by the shareholders by March 17.

- The ex-dividend date for the dividend is February 25 (usually two days before the holder-of-record date). That means that investors who purchase Pepsi shares on or after February 25 do not have the right to receive the dividend.

- On March 17, the payment date, Pepsi deposits or mails dividend checks to the holders of record.

---

3 G.M. Frankfurter, "What Is the Puzzle in 'The Dividend Puzzle?'" *The Journal of Investing,* 8 (1999): 76–85.

A Brief History of Corporate Dividends

During the late 1930s and 1940s, dividends were commonplace among public companies. They were considered the key benefit of stock ownership: Wary investors who had suffered great losses after the 1929 crash demanded higher dividends to offset the risk of holding stock. In fact, the average dividend yield on stocks exceeded 4 percent from 1929 until 1958. During that span, stocks always paid more than bonds. In many years, dividend payments averaged well over 5%.

During the late 1950s, bond yields began to climb and dividend yields dropped due to a combination of factors. First, rising inflation lifted interest rates on a ten-year U.S. Treasury note from 2.3 percent at the beginning of the decade to 4.7 percent by its end. This made bonds more attractive to investors than stocks.

At the same time, the Dow continued its rise after exiting the secular bear market in 1954. The average yield of a Dow stock in 1954 was 4.5 percent.[4] As Dow stock prices increased, their dividend yields (as a percentage of price) dropped below that of bonds. By the end of the decade, the average yield had dropped to 3.3 percent. The average yield of a Dow stock did not rise above 4 percent again until 1974.

In 1960, more than 70 percent of public companies trading on US exchanges paid dividends. Slowly, the number of dividend-paying firms began to wither. Although the companies in the Dow have always paid dividends, by 1999, only 20.8 percent of NYSE and NASDAQ listed firms paid them. The same year marked the end of one of the greatest secular bull markets in stock-market history.

In a 2001 journal article, economists Eugene Fama and

---

4 *Ibbotson SBBI 2015 Classic Yearbook: Market Results for Stocks, Bonds, Bills, and Inflation*, Morningstar: Chicago (2015).

Kenneth French postulated this decline in dividend popularity occurred largely because so many new publicly traded firms were very growth oriented.[5] These firms had a lot in common—small size, low earnings, and large investments relative to earnings—and generally paid few or no dividends. None of these types of firms trade on the Dow, which is reserved for larger blue-chip companies.

More recently, dividend initiations and increases have been positive and today nearly half the firms in the more expensive S&P 500 pay dividends over 2 percent (Table 2.3).

S&P 500 Index Sector	Number of Stocks	Sector Weight in Index	Number of Stocks with Dividends <2%	Median 5-Year Annual Dividend Growth Rate
Consumer Discretionary	82	11.5%	34	8%
Consumer Staples	42	10.9%	28	9%
Energy	43	11.1%	11	8%
Financials	81	15.8%	47	1%
Healthcare	53	12.3%	14	8%
Industrials	60	10.3%	30	8%
Materials	30	3.5%	14	4%
Technology	70	18.2%	28	12%
Telecommunications	8	3.0%	5	3%
Utilities	31	3.4%	29	3%
Totals	500	100%	240	6%

Table 2.3: Stock Yields by Sector, Dividends Over 2 Percent
Source: Thomson Reuters, as of 3/31/2016

There has been another notable change in the dividend climate: a marked increase in the concentration of dividends by payers. In

---

5 E. Fama and K. French, "Disappearing Dividends: Changing Firm Characteristics or Lower Propensity to Pay?" *Journal of Financial Economics,* 60 (2001a): 3–43.

a 2004 journal article,[6] Harry DeAngelo, Linda DeAngelo, and Douglas Skinner found a strong increase in the concentration of dividend payments over the preceding thirty years. While the number of firms that paid dividends steadily declined, the total amount of dividends paid rose in real terms, adjusted for inflation. According to the article, the top twenty-five dividend payers in 2004 accounted for more than half of all dividend payments by public nonfinancial firms.

Astute investors who understand the power of dividends during secular bear markets strongly prefer higher-yield dividend payers. This is especially true in a low-yield environment, where many dividend yields come in above those of US Treasury bonds. That brings us to another bonus offered by dividend-paying stocks: enhanced safety. During times of market turmoil, dividend stocks don't fall as much as others. The relative risk of stock price free-fall—known as downside risk—is measurable through a statistic known as the downside capture ratio.

Downside capture ratio is a statistical measure of overall performance in a down stock market. In a falling stock market, an investment category, or investment manager, with a downside capture ratio below 100 has outperformed the index. For example, a downside capture ratio of 80 indicates that the portfolio measure declined only 80 percent as much as the index during the period. Since 1926, the downside capture ratio of high-dividend-yielding stocks has been 81 percent or lower over various long-term periods (Table 2.4). Perhaps it makes more sense to explain the inverse: Over long-term periods, high-dividend-yielding stocks declined 19 percent less than the broader market.

---

6 H. DeAngelo, L. DeAngelo, and D. Skinner, "Are Dividends Disappearing? Dividend Concentration and the Consolidation of Earnings," *Journal of Financial Economics,* 72 (2004): 425–456.

Time Period	Downside Capture Ratio (The Lower, The Better)
Since 1927	81.53
50-year	67.45
30-year	65.86
20-year	65.83
10-year	81.61

Table 2.4: Downside Capture Ratios of High-Dividend Stocks, 1926–2011
Source: Kenneth French, as of 12/31/2011

In addition to safety, another important benefit of owning dividend-paying stocks during secular bear markets is the consistent increases in dividend payouts. For example, companies in the Dow in the long secular bear market of 1966 to 1982 actually increased dividend payouts by nearly 5 percent per year. If you had invested $100,000 in the Dow in January 1966, on a price basis alone the value of your initial shares would have declined to $90,275 by November 1982. However, by collecting and reinvesting your dividends, you would have acquired more shares while prices had stagnated or fell (i.e., 1972, when the Dow dropped by more than 40 percent).

Stock markets go through more elongated cycles of underperformance than outperformance. By investing in dividend-paying stocks and reinvesting the proceeds, investors can better insulate themselves from treacherous market periods. In the next chapter, I will explore some examples of the promise of dividend reinvestment.

CHAPTER 3

THE SNOWBALL EFFECT: THE PROMISE OF REINVESTING INCOME

"I don't like stock buybacks. I think if a company has the money to buy their stock back, then they should take that and increase the dividends. Send it back to the stockholder. Let them invest their money again from the dividends."

—T. Boone Pickens–

BUILDING A PORTFOLIO with dividends and interest as its bedrock is a long journey. Staying the course through secular bear markets and holding investments that pay dividends is of paramount importance, and many investors today are abandoning a key investment strategy that allows compounding to work.

In 2016, as the Dow once again drew close to its record high of 18,000, slightly more than half of Americans (52 percent) polled by Gallup reported that they currently had money in the stock market (Figure 3.1). That matches the lowest ownership rate in the poll's nineteen-year history. The percentage of Americans who own stocks has been falling steadily since the financial crisis began.

Stock ownership by US investors peaked at 65 percent in 2007. It has been below 60 percent since 2009, even as the broader market has bounced back from its March 2009 lows. Despite recent stock market highs, individual investors remain wary of stocks. More than three in four Americans (76 percent) say they are reluctant to invest in the stock market, even with interest rates on savings accounts and certificates of deposit (CDs) lingering at record lows. Americans' also have a preference for real estate. Already Americans' top pick as the "best long-term investment" for the last two years, Gallup found that real estate has increased its lead over stocks again. Thirty-five percent of Americans now choose real estate compared with a mere 22 percent for stocks and stock mutual funds. But investing in real estate is no panacea. According to the Federal Housing Finance Agency (FHFA), an investment in the average home (as tracked by the Home Price Index from the FHFA) would have grown from $100 in 1975 to nearly $500 by 2013. A similar $100 investment in the Dow, with reinvested dividends, over that time frame would have grown to approximately $1,500. Thus if American investors knew about the power of dividends and reinvestment that stocks can provide, they would likely consider stocks in a different light.

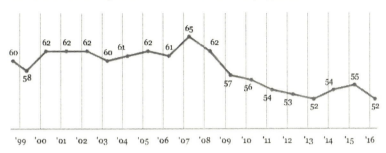

Percentage of U.S. Adults Invested in the Stock Market

Do you, personally, or jointly with a spouse, have any money invested in the stock market right now --
either in an individual stock, a stock mutual fund or in a self-directed 401(k) or IRA?

Selected trends closest to April for each year, from Gallup's annual Economy and Personal Finance survey

GALLUP'

Figure 3.1: Percentage of US Adults Invested in the Stock Market
Source: Gallup, 2016[7]

The fact is that Americans' appetite for risk taking has been short-circuited. Prior to the Internet and housing bubbles of the early and mid-2000s, investing used to be all about taking on risk in order to make money. But today, investors are much more concerned about losing money than making it. The 2008 financial crisis made us all very aware that the financial world of today is much more dangerous than it was twenty years ago. Americans may claim that real estate is the best item to own over the next several years, but the numbers tell a different story. Cash hoarding is rampant: A record $10.1 trillion—more than enough cash to easily buy all thirty Dow companies—is currently parked in money-market mutual funds, bank savings accounts, and certificates of deposit (CDs).[8]

---

7 Gallup, http://www.gallup.com/poll/190883/half-americans-own-stocks-matching-record-low.aspx?g_source=stock%20market&g_medium=search&g_campaign=tiles (accessed May 10, 2016).

8 Stradley & Ranon, Crane Data, Money Market Reform Presentation, 2015.

Unfortunately, all that money sitting in low-risk accounts is effectively earning a return of zero—and when you take inflation into consideration, the real rate of return is actually negative. Main Street investors started lightening up on stocks after the 2008 financial crisis. In the four years ending in 2011, individual investors yanked more than $395 billion out of stock mutual funds, according to the Investment Company Institute.[9]

Investors began to tiptoe back into stock mutual funds again in 2013, adding $185 billion in that year and 2014. However, in 2015, investors again began to withdraw money from mutual funds,by just more than $60 billion.

Not surprisingly, the timing of individual investors' forays into and out of the stock markets has usually been poor. According to a long-running study[10] by Dalbar Associates, a financial consulting firm, during the twenty-year period ending in 2014, investors that were surveyed earned slightly more than 5 percent annually. During the same period, the Dow averaged a 9.95 percent return when dividend reinvestment is taken into consideration.

This remarkable gap in performance is largely attributable to investors' efforts to time the market and avoid dividend stocks. For example, during the 2008 market crash, the average investor surveyed by Dalbar lost 24 percent of his or her portfolio value, compared to an 18.4 percent drop for the Dow. This evidence strongly

---

9 Adam Shell, "Financial crisis ushers in 'The Age of Safety' for investors," USA Today, September 4, 2012. Accessed at: http://usatoday30.usatoday.com/money/markets/story/2012-09-04/investing-stocks-safety-risk/57582840/1, May 28, 2016

10 John F. Wasik, "Retirement Investors, Riding Out the Panic," New York Times, October 9, 2015. Accessed at: http://www.nytimes.com/2015/10/11/business/mutfund/retirement-investors-riding-out-the-panic.html?_r=0, May 28, 2016.

suggests that individual investors are very poor market timers and stock selectors. I have no doubt, however, that the fear of owning stocks through secular bear periods like the Great Recession would be reduced if investors stayed put in the markets and focused less on price and more on dividend income and the power of compounding.

Let's take a look at the power of compounding by examining an investment in Pepsi. Pepsi, one of the largest companies in the world, is a global firm that maintains a high level of cash generation and ample dividends. The key to owning stock in companies like Pepsi is not the stock's daily price performance, but the cash the company allocates to its shareholders.

Consider an investor who earmarked $100,000 of her retirement portfolio to Pepsi right at the end of the last secular bull market, 2000. For simplicity's sake, I've rendered the information in Table 3.1 by showing the proceeds from the $100,000 initial investment in Pepsi shares in 2000 and then at the end of each subsequent year.

The investor began with 2,680 shares of Pepsi from her initial $100,000 investment. During the first year of investment, she received $1,500.80 in dividends. She could—and did—choose to use the proceeds of these dividends to purchase forty more shares of Pepsi at the end of the year. Each year, her number of shares grew, and the dividends she received were reinvested.

Date	Shares Held	Annual Dividend	Price (PEP)	Dividend Pay-out for Last 12 Months	Shares Repur-chased	Value + Cash Remain-der
12/31/2000	2,680	$0.56	$37.29	$1,500.80	40	$62.80
12/31/2001	2,720	$0.58	$37.08	$1,577.60	44	$8.88
12/31/2002	2,764	$0.60	$32.58	$1,658.40	51	$5.70
12/31/2003	2,815	$0.63	$36.51	$1,773.45	48	$26.67
12/31/2004	2,863	$0.85	$41.55	$2,433.55	58	$50.32
12/30/2005	2,921	$1.01	$47.88	$2,950.21	62	$31.97
12/29/2006	2,983	$1.16	$51.65	$3,460.28	67	$31.70
12/31/2007	3,050	$1.43	$63.98	$4,361.50	68	$42.56
12/31/2008	3,118	$1.60	$47.37	$4,988.80	106	$10.14
12/31/2009	3,224	$1.75	$54.30	$5,642.00	104	$4.94
12/31/2010	3,328	$1.89	$60.10	$6,289.92	104	$44.46
12/30/2011	3,432	$2.03	$62.97	$6,966.96	111	$21.75
Secular Bull Market Resumes						
12/31/2012	3,543	$2.13	$66.99	$7,546.59	112	$65.46
12/31/2013	3,655	$2.24	$82.36	$8,187.20	100	$16.66
12/31/2014	3,755	$2.40	$91.76	$9,012.00	98	$36.18
12/31/2015	3,853	$99.92 Price				

Table 3.1: Pepsi Dividend Reinvestment Example, 2000–2015

The Pepsi investor started her investment program in 2000 with 2,680 shares of stock. By the end of the secular bear market in 2011 she held 3,432 shares of stock. Her portfolio had more than doubled over that period of stagnation. I continued the example through the end of 2015. By then, she had accumulated 3,853 shares. One of the key elements to the growth in her portfolio was dividend enhancement each year. Throughout the period of her investment, Pepsi continued to advance its dividend substantially: In 2000, the yearly dividend was $0.56 per share, but by the end of 2015, the dividend had risen to $2.40 per share and was expected to be $2.80 per share in 2016.

Since the investor owned 3,853 shares of Pepsi in 2015 thanks to her stock repurchasing plan, her total net portfolio on December 31, 2015 was $384,606—almost four times her initial investment. There are several noteworthy points about this exercise:

- Dividend growth is just as important as the yield paid at the initial stock investment. The power of compounding is enhanced through rising dividend payments. The more shares you own and the higher the annual dividend rises in the future, the better the compounding effect works in your favor.

- When the stock market goes through difficult periods, such as it did in 2008, an investor focused on building wealth through the compounding effect of dividend reinvestment comes out ahead. The reason: If prices fall, it simply means that the investor can buy more shares.

- Examine the amount of shares repurchased at the end of 2008 versus 2007 in Table 3.2. The Pepsi investor was able to purchase 106 shares of Pepsi stock with dividend proceeds at the end of 2008—substantially more than the previous year's repurchase of 68 shares. When Pepsi's share price dropped, the investor was able to purchase more shares when she reinvested her dividends. It may seem counterintuitive, but a temporary drop in price for a dividend-yielding stock an investor owns is a benefit, as it allows her to buy more shares.

Date	Shares Held	Annual Dividend	Price (PEP)	Dividend Payout for Last 12 Months	Shares Repurchased	Value + Cash Remainder
12/31/2007	3,050	$1.43	$ 63.98	$4,361.50	68	$42.56
12/31/2008	3,118	$1.60	$ 47.37	$4,988.80	106	$10.14

Table 3.2: Pepsi Dividend Reinvestment Example, 2007–2008

- Investors focused on building wealth through adding shares by reinvestment must overlook periods of extreme market volatility and not be frightened away from the stock market in secular bear markets. An erudite investor who chooses to stay with a dividend reinvestment program through thick and thin will be rewarded.

Pepsi is an example of a stock that has appreciated in price since the Internet bubble of 2000. Now, we'll examine a company whose stock fell in price during the entire 15 year period, but continued to expand its dividend and reward its shareholders: Northern Trust, one of the largest trust banks in the United States. Table 3.3 shows how an investor would have fared at the end of 2015 based on an initial investment of $100,000 in Northern Trust at the end of year 2000 with a starting price of $81.91.

Date	Shares Held	Annual Dividend	Price (NTRS)	Dividend Pay-out for Last 12 Months	Shares Re-purchased	Value + Cash Re-mainder
12/31/2000	1,220	0.54	$81.91	$658.80	8	$62.80
12/31/2001	1,228	0.62	$60.70	$761.36	12	$62.08
12/31/2002	1,240	0.68	$35.05	$ 843.20	24	$42.27
12/31/2003	1,264	0.68	$46.00	$ 859.52	18	$56.47
12/31/2004	1,282	0.76	$48.73	$ 974.32	19	$71.25
12/30/2005	1,301	0.84	$51.72	$1,092.84	21	$73.53
12/29/2006	1,322	0.94	$61.07	$1,242.68	10	$65.06
12/31/2007	1,332	1.03	$76.38	$1,371.96	17	$23.50
12/31/2008	1,349	1.12	$50.52	$1,510.88	29	$61.78
12/31/2009	1,378	1.12	$52.84	$1,543.36	29	$46.06
12/31/2010	1,407	1.12	$55.35	$1,575.84	28	$23.14
12/30/2011	1,435	1.12	$40.03	$1,607.20	40	$43.07
12/31/2012	1,475	1.18	$50.02	$1,740.50	34	$57.63
12/31/2013	1,509	1.30	$48.95	$1,961.70	40	$77.28
12/31/2014	1,549	1.44	$64.41	$2,230.56	34	$80.67
12/31/2015	1,573	$72.09 Price				

Table 3.3: Northern Trust Dividend Reinvestment Example, 2000–2015

The investor in this example collected $17,744 in dividends over the fifteen-year time period. Because he chose to reinvest those dividends, his share count grew from 1,220 to 1,573. Without dividend payments or reinvestment, he would have lost more than 10 percent on the Northern Trust stock investment, as the price fell from $81.91 to $72.09 over the period of 2000-2015. His investment would have been worth $87,949.80 if Northern Trust did not pay dividends, instead of $113,397.57 with the actual dividend payments and reinvestment.

This proves that even in the most difficult of secular bear markets, a dividend investor keeps capital losses to a minimum. Remember, at the initial starting period of ownership, Northern Trust was paying out $658.80 on the original $100,000 investment—an annual yield of less than 1 percent. But by the end of 2015, the investor was receiving $2,230.56 in cash dividends from the original investment of $100,000—more than three times greater than his initial yield.

Selecting Dividend-Paying Stocks

- Choose firms with a solid history of dividend payments plus above-average dividend growth. I generally seek a minimum of 5 percent in dividend growth rate for prospective investments. As I mentioned in the Pepsi example, the snowball effect of dividend payments *plus* the rate of dividend growth ultimately enriches investors.

- Choose firms with moderate dividend payout ratios. Firms with moderate or even low payout ratios will have the financial capacity to continue paying and raising dividends at an above-market rate.

> · Choose firms with an above-average dividend yield based on their price and dividend history. Firms that trade at low dividend/payout ratios offer investors an opportunity for added appreciation through share price and dividend reinvestment.

Year	2006	2007	2008	2009	2010	2011	2012
Dividend Per Share	$1.16	$1.43	$1.60	$1.75	$1.89	$2.03	$2.13
Dividend/ Payout Ratio	37%	40%	49%	46%	47%	49%	53%
Dividend Yield Avg.	1.9%	2.1%	2.4%	3.2%	2.9%	3.1%	3.1%
Dividend Growth Rate	14.85%	23.28%	11.89%	9.37%	8.00%	7.41%	4.93%
Stock Price High/Low	$56–$66	$62–$79	$50–$80	$44–$65	$59–$68	$59–$72	$62–$74
Dividend Yield Percentage High/Low	1.6%–2.1%	1.8%–2.3%	2.0%–3.2%	2.7%–4.0%	2.7%–3.3%	2.8%–3.5%	2.8%–3.5%
Valuation	Over	Over	Under	Under	Under	Under	Under

Table 3.4: Pepsi Dividend/Price Analysis, 2006–2012

As you can see in Table 3.4, Pepsi shares traded at a range of $44 per share to $80 per share over the six-year period as Pepsi's dividend continued to advance. The dividend yield percentage high/low, or current yield, fluctuated between 1.6 percent and 4 percent. On a dividend-to-share-price basis, Pepsi is most undervalued when its current yield nears 4 percent and most overvalued, based on historical precedent, when its current yield falls below to 2 percent.

Pepsi's ability to advance dividends slowed to only 5 percent in 2012, far below its historical rate. A slower dividend growth rate ultimately leads to reduced reinvestment of Pepsi dividends in the future. As Pepsi is now paying more than 50 percent of its earnings in dividends (the dividend payout ratio), future dividend increases will most likely trend slightly below earnings growth.

Clearly, Pepsi was a tremendous investment from 2000 to 2015. As of April 2016, Pepsi's current yield was 2.83 percent, based on the year's dividend ($2.81) compared to its current price ($99.03)—right in the middle of its historical dividend yield range.

If you apply a price-to-dividend ratio analysis to stocks you are thinking of purchasing or already own, you can purchase, or reinvest, cash at optimal points in time. If Pepsi's share price falls and the yield nears 4 percent, the investor could then time her purchases in the most efficient manner and gain the most shares of Pepsi stock possible. Following this type of market timing will allow an investor to collect more shares of a company's stock at the times when it is most undervalued.

CHAPTER 4

THE SMALL-CAP PARADOX

"Great intellects are skeptical."

—Friedrich Wilhelm Nietzche, 1844–1900

L ARGE COMPANY STOCKS, like those within the Dow, often go through periods of elongated stagnation in secular bear markets. Many pundits argue that adding other asset classes to your portfolio can help you offset the risk of underperformance during these times. These assets may include small-cap stocks, gold, bonds, and commodities. This chapter examines small-cap (*cap* is short for capitalization) stocks, which trade at much lower market capitalizations (henceforth, *market cap*) than their larger brethren but can provide income as well. Small-cap stocks do routinely provide dissimilar performance patterns than large-cap stocks, but you might wonder: *Are small-cap stocks a worthwhile investment for me, since I'm planning to concentrate my portfolio on dividend-paying stocks? Can small-cap stocks help me avoid portfolio stagnation during secular bear market periods?*

Before examining the virtues of small-cap stocks, I must first define the term *small cap*. Market cap is the number of shares outstanding in a company multiplied by the share's price. A company with a billion shares outstanding and a share price of $50 would have a market cap of $50 billion—a large-cap stock. A company with a million shares outstanding and a share price of $50 would have a market cap of $50 million—a small-cap stock.

Note that in this example, the price per share is the same. While it is true that small-cap stocks sometimes, and even often, have a lower price per share than large-cap stocks, it is not *always* true. Price per share has no bearing on whether a stock is small cap or large cap. The definition of a small-cap stock is imprecise, but I use $1 billion as a benchmark and consider any company trading below this market cap a small cap.

The line is drawn differently elsewhere. Most academic researchers suggest that small caps must be far below a $1 billion market cap to capture the desired diversification effect. These "smallest of the small caps" are sometimes referred to as *micro-cap stocks*.

Why is market cap important? Because history has shown that stocks of companies with different market caps behave differently in terms of return and risk. Several older academic studies have concluded that over long periods of time, the stocks of small companies have outperformed those of larger ones. This occurs because small company stocks have a so-called risk premium—because they are riskier, investors should be compensated with higher returns.

Why are they riskier? Most small-cap companies are in the early years of their evolution. While they gain maturity, they have limited reserves for hard times. Also, if a smaller company loses a few key executives, or if the economy takes a turn for the worse, it only takes a few nervous investors to cause the stock to plummet.

Most financial planners and market commentators have recommended for years that small-cap shares be a part of every diversified portfolio, largely due to their performance attributes and theoretical risk reduction. I believe, however, that a small-cap paradox exists. Consider the following facts:

- Small caps have undergone substantial periods of under-performance and their own unique secular bear market periods, especially during the last thirty years.

- Institutions are now becoming more dominant in the capital markets.

- Small caps have a high level of volatility and downside risk.

- Fewer small-cap firms pay dividend yields above 2 percent—the key element for an investor to withstand a secular bear market.

THE SIZE-EFFECT PHENOMENON

The small-firm effect was first discovered by the general public over thirty years ago. In a widely known academic journal article in the early 1980s, Rolf Banz published some of the most important research ever written on the so-called small-firm effect. In the study,[11] Banz separated all New York Stock Exchange stocks into quantization (shares outstanding multiplied by stock price) and examined their returns; he found that the average annual gain of the smallest firms was almost 20 percent higher than that of the largest firms. Banz's documentation of the small-firm effect spawned many subsequent academic papers. In fact, a special issue of the *Journal of Financial Economics* that was devoted to small caps contained several papers that added to the canon of literature on the size effect.

One early vital discovery about small-cap stocks was made by Donald B. Keim. He demonstrated in a 1983 study that nearly

---

11 R. Banz, "The Relationship between Return and Market Value of Common Stocks," *Journal of Financial Economics,* (1981), 9(1): 3–18.

50 percent of the average outperformance during the period from 1963 occurred in the month of January. Additionally, Keim observed, more than one-quarter of all excess returns came in the first week of January alone.[12] This is often ascribed to the notion that some investors sell their securities at the end of the calendar year in order to establish capital losses for income tax purposes. These waves of stock sales can put downward pressure on security prices at the end of year.[13] But then conversely, it causes upward pressure on shares in January after all the selling is exhausted.

In addition to the Keim data, one detail has always been in question. For six straight years between 1975 and 1981; small-cap stocks had an <u>average annual increase</u> of more than 35 percent. This six-year surge was largely responsible for a preponderance of early journal articles crowing about how small-cap stocks historically outperform large-cap stocks. Since this six-year run of supreme outperformance, the annualized returns of small-cap stocks has not been as stellar. During multiple periods since 1981, small-cap stocks have dramatically underperformed large-cap stocks (Table 4.1). The Russell 2000 Index, which is the most commonly referenced US small-cap index, began in 1978, and the Russell 1000 Index is its large-cap corollary. During the seven-year period from 1984 to 1991, small-cap (as measured by the Russell 2000 Index) stocks returned a pedestrian 4.6 percent on an annual basis versus 13.7 percent for large-cap stocks. From 1995 through the end of 1999, small-cap stocks had an annualized return of 10.2 percent

---

12 Donald B. Keim, "Size-Related Anomalies and Stock Return Seasonality," *Journal of Financial Economics,* (1983), 12: 13–32.

13 Kathryn E. Easterday, Pradyot K. Sen, and Jens A. Stephan, "The Persistence of the Small Firm/January Effect: Is It Consistent with Investors' Learning and Arbitrage Efforts?" *The Quarterly Review of Economics and Finance,* 49 (2009), 1172–1193.

versus 18.3 percent for large caps. In addition, in the past three-, five-, and ten-year intervals, large-cap stocks continued to outperform small caps (Table 4.2).

Period	Small Cap	Large Cap
1984–1991	4.6%	13.7%
1995–1999	10.2%	18.3%
2005–2008	-3.6%	-2.8%
2012–2015	7.2%	12.2%

Table 4.1: Small Cap versus Large Cap Underperformance, 1984–2015
Source: Russell Corporation, through 12/31/2015

Period	Small Cap	Large Cap
3 years	7.2%	12.2%
5 years	6.8%	13.1%
10 years	5.4%	6.7%

Table 4.2: Small Cap versus Large Cap Underperformance, Various Ranges
Source: Russell Corporation, through 12/31/2015

According to data from Russell, a $100,000 investment in small-cap US stocks at the end of 1978 would have grown to $370,597 by the end of 2015. This compares unfavorably to the $598,344 outcome with a similar investment in large-cap US stocks.

Clearly, the positive small-size effect postulated by Banz in his famous 1981 study has been slowly eroding over the last few decades, and several academic studies have chronicled this fact. Julia Sawicki, Nilanjan Sen, and Cheah Chee Yian of Nenyang University revisited the small-cap effect twenty-five years after the Banz study was published and found it to be positive only during that 1975 to 1983 period.[14] The authors hypothesized that small-cap firms may have indeed have held a narrow lead in performance prior to 1980,

---

14 Julia Sawicki, Nilanjan Sen, and Cheah Chee Yian, "The Disappearance of the Small Stock Premium: Size as a Narrowly-Held Risk," 2005, 19-22.

but once the advantage was well promoted (during the 1980s and 1990s), the size effect began to vanish.

Another researcher, John Campbell of Harvard University, suggested that the small-cap advantage may be simply a "mistake" [15] that was corrected once investors learned of the small-cap bias. He argued that the glacial process of individual investor learning and industry innovations (e.g., small-cap mutual funds) enabled more investors to participate in small stocks over time.

A recent paper by Cliff Asness [16] also held a cynical view of small caps. According to the author, small caps have a weak historical record that varies significantly over time—one that became particularly weak after its popularization in the early 1980s. The author concluded that the premium is solely concentrated among micro-cap stocks (smallest of the small), that the premium predominantly "resides in January," that it is "weak internationally," and "is subsumed by proxies for illiquidity." [17]

I believe the explanation is quite simple: As new investors entered small-cap stocks over the past three decades, the risk inherent in these types of securities became more widely shared—and thus the excess returns started to evaporate. In the periods when small caps did outperform large caps, the illiquid micro-cap stocks included in the group seem to have driven a noteworthy segment of the performance gap. This suggests that the small-cap premium may actually be

---

15 John Y. Campbell, "Asset Pricing at the Millennium," *Journal of Finance*, 55 (2000): 1515–1567.

16 Cliff Asness, Andrea Frazzini, Ronen Israel, Tobias Maskowitz, and Lasse Pedersen. "Size Matters If You Control the Junk," working paper, 2015, 55-59.

17 Ibid, abstract.

compensation for liquidity risk. A few studies have presented direct evidence that liquidity risk helped explain the small-cap premium.[18]

An alternative interpretation of the disappearance of the small-cap size effect was offered by author Jeremy Siegel, who suggested that the high cost of transactions with small-cap stocks effected performance.[19] Donald B. Keim also found that the transaction costs are substantial. Keim and his coauthor Gabriel Hawakini examined the total costs of trading—not only commissions and bid-asked spreads, but also the effect of trading on the prices of securities being bought or sold—between 1991 and 1993.[20] They found that total trading costs for the buying and selling of the smallest stocks were sometimes above 7 percent. Another study by Kabir Hassan in 2004 found that once transaction costs are considered, small firms offer no positive abnormal returns over large cap stocks.[21]

Another area of dispute is the data held on small-cap stocks by the The Center for Research in Security Prices (CRSP). The CRSP database fails to account for stocks delisted by stock exchanges for performance-related reasons. The CRSP simply ignores these stocks in its calculations, rather than gathering their new, depressingly low prices and computing their returns. As a result, many researchers conclude the CRSP overstates performance. Academic

18 Weimin Liu,"A Liquidity-Augmented Capital Asset Pricing Model," *Journal of Financial Economics,* 82(3) (2006): 631–671.

19 Jeremy J. Siegel, *Stocks for the Long Run* (New York: McGraw-Hill, 2002), 78-80.

20 Gabriel Hawakini and Donald B. Keim, "The Cross Section of Common Stock Returns: A Review of the Evidence and Some New Findings," Rodney L. White Center for Financial Research, Wharton School: 1999.

21 S. al Rjoub and M.K. Hassan, "Transaction Cost and the Small Stock Puzzle: The Impact of Outliers in the NYSE, 1970–2000," *International Journal of Applied Econometrics and Quantitative Studies,* 1(3) (2004), 103–114.

studies examining this phenomenon have concluded that NASDAQ-delisted stocks could affect the long-term investment results of small caps by as much as 3 percent.

THE IMPACT OF INSTITUTIONS

Small-cap stocks are also unpopular with institutional investors, such as pensions and mutual funds—which is clearly problematic, given the fact that the institutional market is growing rapidly. Today, large institutional investors hold a large percentage of the country's equities, and they prefer to buy large-cap stocks. (Often, this is because institutions have mandates on market limitations and risk concentrations.) Many pundits argue that the relative weakness of small-cap stocks since 1982 can also be blamed on the growth of institutional investors, and indeed, it does appear to have some effect. Evidence suggests that the growing power of institutions is having an adverse effect on the ability of smaller, financially sound companies to obtain investor recognition.

Economists Paul Gompers and Andrew Metrick,[22] who are faculty research fellows at the National Bureau of Economic Research, arrived at that conclusion after correlating patterns with stocks and institutions. From disclosure statements, they found that institutions managing at least $100 million of securities raised their percentage of the equity market from 26 percent in 1980 to 51 percent in 1996. Jonathan Lewellen of Dartmouth College found that this had risen to 62 percent by 2005.[23] Lewellen also found that from

---

22 P.A. Gompers and A. Metrick, "Institutional Investors and Equity Prices," *Quarterly Journal of Economics,* 116 (2001), 229–259.

23 Jonathan Lewellen, "Institutional Investors and the Limits of Arbitrage," *Journal of Financial Economics,* 102(1) (2011), 63-64.

1980 to 2005, institutions tilted toward large-cap stocks, with 77 percent of a typical institutional portfolio devoted to large caps.

Not only have institutions come to own more of the country's equities than ever before, they also lean toward the largest of the blue-chip stocks, mostly because of policy restrictions and the size of the assets within the funds. Institutional investors are often forbidden from owning more than 5 percent of a company's shares, a limitation that's easy to follow when investing in Microsoft. Of course, this confines the institutions to focus on large, liquid stocks.

Also, a small company rarely gets considered as an investment by institutions simply because a large fund purchase of its shares would have an inordinate affect on the company's share price. Plus, if an institution wanted to take a large position in the small-cap company's stock—say, 3 percent—it would have to take a large public stake in it.

DOWNSIDE RISK

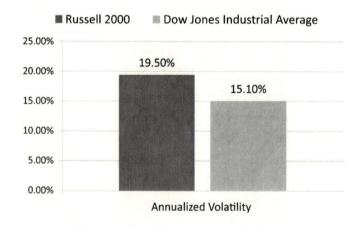

Figure 4.1: Volatility: 1979–2015
Source: Russell Corporation, Standard & Poor's, through 12/31/2015

Small caps are inherently more volatile. The average standard deviation of the Russell 2000 Index since 1979 is 19.5 percent, versus 15.1 percent for the Dow. The chance of dramatic capital loss from small caps is also higher than from large caps. When large caps declined in 1973 by 14.7 percent, small caps dropped 30.9 percent. In the crash of 1987, large caps dropped 30.7 percent but small caps sank 38.2 percent. Thus small-cap stocks almost always will bear a heavier burden of a market decline.

THE PARADOX OF SMALL CAPS

If small-cap stocks are more volatile and maintain a lower overall total return than large caps, should income investors consider them? This is the paradox. One consideration for any asset class is its correlation, or the statistical measure of how two securities move in relation to each other. The lower the correlation, the more attractive the additional asset will be in providing diversification to a portfolio.

The correlation between small- and large-cap companies has averaged .81 in the twenty-year period ending December 31, 2015, but of late, correlations have been increasing. According to data from Charles Schwab, small caps had a correlation to large caps of .66 from 1995 to 2000. From 2001 to 2007, this increased to .83, and from 2008 to 2014, to .94. This phenomenon is not limited to small caps, as many other equity asset classes (including international) followed the same pattern.

Small-cap stocks are also infrequently dividend payers. Of the 4,234 companies in the Russell 2000 Index, only 1,363 pay dividends. Of these, 875 pay dividends of 2 percent or higher—my preferred requirement for investing in a dividend stock. If an investor is considering small-cap stocks as part of a diversified portfolio, the universe is therefore limited.

If an investor is to consider investing in small-cap stocks, only dividend-paying firms should be considered. Analysis in 2015 by Royce Research[24] found that dividend-paying companies within the Russell 2000 measured well relative to their nonpaying counterparts from December 31, 1992 through December 31, 2014. The average annual total return for the twenty-two–year period was 11.2 percent for small-cap dividend payers versus 8.2 percent for nonpaying firms. This compares favorably to the 9.5 percent annual return for the small-cap index itself and nearly matches the large-cap index.

Unsurprisingly, the index's dividend-paying small-cap companies showed higher returns in thirteen of the twenty-two calendar-year periods examined. Outperformance in five out of seven down-market calendar-year periods was a major contributor to the positive performance of dividend-paying small-cap companies. Small-cap dividend firms also maintain a low downside capture ratio, just like their large-cap brethren.

The conventional wisdom has always been that because small caps possess higher risks, their returns should inevitably be higher. That's nonsense. Data prove that small-cap stocks have *not* outperformed large-cap stocks since 1979. Data on the long-term returns of small caps going back to 1926 are also highly suspect, considering the extreme performance advantage of the 1976–1983 period.

THE MICRO-CAP ADVANTAGE

The micro-cap segment of the US markets is a very small piece of the greater small-cap universe. The aggregate market capitalization of the entire micro-cap class is just over $200 billion in investable

---

24 The Royce Funds, "The Importance of Small-Cap Investing," https://www.roycefunds.com/insights/whitepapers/dividends-crucial-component-long-term-investment-approach (accessed April 27, 2016).

assets—the same size as a single Dow firm, Pfizer. Micro-caps are the smallest firms in the small-cap category; the average market capitalization of companies in the micro-cap universe is about $300 million. For many years, the investment industry lacked a clear definition of the difference between small-cap and micro-cap stocks.

When Russell began publishing the Russell Microcap Index in June 2005 (including data back tested to 2000), it became the first to offer up a formal definition and an industry categorization standard. The Russell Microcap Index includes about 1,000 of the smallest securities in the Russell 2000 Index by market capitalization. Russell then combines those stocks with another 1,000 securities in the small-cap universe that are considered to be illiquid.

Today, the average market capitalization in the Russell Microcap Index is just over $400 million—quite a bit smaller than the average $1.8 billion of companies in the Russell 2000 Index. Russell Microcap Index stocks are inherently illiquid, which means that for daily trading, shares are measured in thousands rather than millions. It is thus more difficult for an investor to trade these types of stocks.

However, the advantage of micro-cap stocks is their correlation to the larger-cap Dow—about .65, much lower than the entire small-cap universe. Furthermore, since 2008, the correlation has steadily been decreasing—the opposite of what is happening in the broader Russell 2000 Index. This provides better diversification for investors. Although the universe of dividend-paying micro caps is also small, a few hundred firms do offer investors compelling yields.

The micro-cap universe contains about 1,300 firms, and I've provided a list in the appendix of nearly 100 micro-cap stocks that pay solid dividend yields. You can sort through this list to find promising candidates for direct investment or invest in a micro-cap fund that includes firms in the list. There are two caveats in investing in micro-cap stocks individually. The first is research. Micro-caps have far less information available to investors and research reports from the major brokerage firms are rare. Secondly, there is the illiquidity issue. The bid/ask spreads for micro-cap companies will be much higher than larger firms that trade millions of shares per day. So although I find the merits of micro-cap stocks with solid dividends compelling, investing most of your portfolio in larger-cap dividend firms makes the most sense.

CHAPTER 5

THE POWER OF BOND INTEREST

"Compound interest is the eighth wonder of the world ... the greatest mathematical discovery of our time."

—Mark Twain, 1835–1910

WHAT ARE BONDS?

S O FAR, I'VE proven that the notion "stocks always go up" is a falsehood. I've also proven that even during extended periods of underperformance for stocks, investors who place their hard-earned dollars into high-yielding dividend stocks—like Pepsi, for example—can still earn moderate returns.

But there are other options for investors during secular bear stock markets. Many investors consider bonds boring and a poor alternative to other investment choices. Yet they provide great potential in terms of diversification and offer dependable semi-annual income during the elongated periods when stocks stagnate.

A bond is a debt security—it is analogous to an I.O.U. When you purchase a bond, you are lending money to a government, corporation, municipality, or other entity known in the bond world as the *issuer*. In return for the money you lend, the issuer promises to pay you back a stated rate of interest during the life of the bond and ultimately repay the bond's face value upon its maturation date (the end date of the bond).

Most investors put their money in bonds for diversification and safety. The price you pay for a bond is based on a multitude of variables, including prevailing interest rates, liquidity, credit quality, maturity and tax status.

THE LANGUAGE OF BONDS

Newly issued bonds normally sell at or close to *par value*, which means 100 percent of the *face*, or *principal*, value. Previously issued bonds trade on secondary markets and can vary widely in price. Secondary bonds fluctuate in price in response to changes in interest rates, credit quality, wide-ranging economic conditions, and supply and demand. When a bond's price increases above its face value, it is considered to be *selling at a premium*. A bond selling below face value is considered to be *selling at a discount*.

WHAT'S THE DIFFERENCE BETWEEN A BOND AND A STOCK TRADER? A BOND MATURES.

Bond *interest* can be fixed, floating, or payable at maturity. Most bonds carry a fixed interest rate until maturity that is expressed as a percentage of the principal value. For example, a $1,000 corporate bond with an interest rate of 4 percent will pay the holder $40 per year, or $20 every six months. This $40 interest payment is known as a *coupon*.

A bond's *maturity date* is the specific date on which the investor's principal (the amount of money loaned) will be repaid. Generally, bond terms range from one to thirty years. Term ranges are often categorized as follows:

- Short-term: Maturities of up to five years
- Medium-term: Maturities of five to ten years
- Long-term: Maturities greater than ten years

Investors choose terms based on when they need their initial investment repaid and also on their risk tolerance. Short-term bonds, which generally offer lower interest rates, are considered a fairly safe investment because principal is repaid sooner. Conversely, long-term bonds provide better interest rates in order to compensate investors for potential bond price fluctuations (in the event that the investor decides to sell the bond before maturation) and for locking up their funds for an extended period of time.

While its maturity date indicates how long a bond will be in effect, or *outstanding*, many bonds are designed to allow the issuer to change the maturity date. This *redemption* or *call provision* allows the issuer to redeem the bonds at a specified price and certain time period prior to the bond's maturation. If a bond is *called*, it is redeemed early.

A bond's *yield* is the return earned on the bond based on the price paid and the interest payments the bondholder receives. Typically, yields are quoted in basis points (abbreviated as bps and pronounced "bips"). One basis point is equal to one one-hundredth of a percentage point, or 0.01 percent, so, for example, 4.00 percent = 400 bps.

Current Yield and Yield to Maturity

Investors are usually quoted two types of bond yields: *current yield* and *yield to maturity*. Current yield is the annual return on the dollar amount paid for the bond; it is derived by dividing the bond's interest payment by its purchase price. Thus, a bond purchased at par for $1,000 with an annual interest payment of $40 maintains a current yield of 4 percent. Let's call that Bond A.

However, if the price of the bond in question falls below its original purchase price and trades at a discount to par, the same bond will have a higher current yield. If a $1,000 bond trades for $925, a discount, the current yield would be calculated by the annualized payment ($40) divided by its *current* price ($925), rather than its par value, $1,000. Let's call that Bond B.

In Bond B's case, the current yield would be 4.32 percent. It is important to note that this calculation of current yield does not take into account a critical concept: An investor who holds the discount bond to maturity also collects a capital gain of $75—the difference between the $925 price paid and the bond's $1,000 par value at maturity.

That is why the most important calculation to know in owning bonds is known as yield to maturity. Yield to maturity (YTM) takes this critical maturity value concept into account. It is the preferred measure for bonds, as it considers the price paid for the bond, the coupons collected (interest paid), and maturity at par value. This calculation, which is universal to all bonds, enables an investor to properly compare bonds with different maturities and coupon payments.

As with current yield, YTM is expressed as a percentage. It is hard to calculate a precise YTM, but you can approximate its value by using a bond yield table or one of the many YTM online calculators. Alternately, you can consider using this formula:

Approximate YTM = $(C + ((F - P) \div n)) \div (F + P) \div 2$

In this formula, C = coupon or interest payment; F = face or par value; P = current price of the bond; and n = years to maturity.

Consider the facts of Bond B in the context of this formula: Bond B was priced at a discount, $925, and had a coupon of $40. Its face value was $1,000, and its maturity date was ten years.

Approximate YTM = ($40 + (($1,000 − $925) ÷ 10)) ÷ ($1,000 + $925) ÷ 2

= $47.5 ÷ $962.50 = 4.93 percent

This calculation reveals an approximate YTM of 4.93 percent for Bond B.

Of course, it's much easier to calculate actual YTM using Microsoft Excel or an online calculator. An online calculator determined an actual YTM of 4.97 percent for Bond B—very close to the 4.93 yield determined with the approximate formula. You can find online calculators at Investopedia.com (http://www.investopedia.com/calculator/aoytm.aspx) and Fidelity.com (https://powertools.fidelity.com/fixedincome/yield.do).

YIELD TO CALL

Another key metric of bond return analysis is yield to call, which measures the total return bondholders receive if they hold bonds until they are called at the issuer's discretion. In many cases, issuers pay investors a premium for the right to call bonds before their maturity date. Yield to call is calculated the same way as yield to maturity, but assumes that the bond will be called at some point before maturity.

From the moment a bond is issued until the day it either matures or is called, its price in the marketplace fluctuates depending on the bond's terms and also general market conditions, including prevailing interest rates, the credit quality of the issuer (more on that in a bit), economic conditions, and other factors. Because of the variability of bond prices, a bond's actual value will most likely be higher or lower than its face value if it is sold before it matures or is called.

In general, when interest rates fall, bond prices go up. The inverse is also true: When interest rates rise, bond prices fall. Consider Bond B, which was originally issued with a 4 percent coupon. If interest rates rise to 5 percent during Bond B's term, Bond B's price will fall to approximately $925 so its YTM will remain consistent with the current market yield of 5 percent.

Government bonds are another story. Their prices rise not only when interest rates fall, but also when other assets—such as stocks—take a dive. Perhaps you've heard of the "fear trade." During periods of economic or political crisis, many investors sell riskier assets, like stocks, and put their money in safer investments. US Treasury securities are one such alternative. Prices of government bonds rise in these situations because so much money pours into low-risk assets.

One other item to pay close attention to is accrued interest, the fraction of the coupon payment that bond sellers earn for holding the bond for a period of time between bond payments. Accrued interest is a significant element to consider if investors are contemplating buying bonds on the secondary market.

CREDIT QUALITY

A bond issuer's *credit quality* is the likelihood that it will pay its investors the interest and principal they are due in a timely manner. The spectrum of credit quality ranges from that of US Treasury bonds, which are considered risk free because they are backed by the full faith and credit of the federal government, to speculative bonds. Since a bond's maturity date may be well in the future, credit quality is a vital consideration when evaluating bonds.

When a bond is issued, the issuer must provide details as to its financial soundness and creditworthiness. This information can be found in the *offering document, official statement,* or *prospectus,* which explains the bond's terms and features as well as any risk investors should be aware of before putting their hard earned cash into a bond security.

In the United States, major rating agencies assign ratings to bonds based on their study of the issuer's financial condition and management, economic and debt characteristics, and the precise revenue sources that secure the bonds. These agencies include Moody's Investors Service, Standard & Poor's (S&P) Corporation and Fitch Ratings. The highest ratings are Aaa (Moody's) and AAA (S&P and Fitch Ratings).

Bonds rated in the BBB/Baa category or higher are considered *investment grade*; bonds rated lower than those grades are considered *high yield* or *junk*. A lower rating indicates that a bond is considerably riskier than a highly rated bond. Lower-rated bonds generally have higher interest rates, as greater yield is promised as compensation for the greater risk of default.

Rating agencies make their ratings accessible to the public online through their respective websites. Their ratings are also reported on many independent websites, including Yahoo! Finance and most major brokerage firm sites. In addition, printed versions of their reports and ratings are available in many local libraries.

Rating agencies continuously scrutinize issuers and sometimes change ratings of issuers' bonds based on changing credit factors. Typically, rating agencies will provide a warning sign they are considering a rating change by placing the bond on CreditWatch (S&P), Under Review (Moody's), or Rating Watch (Fitch Ratings).

Investors should remember that ratings are judgments. In the past, credit ratings have been a fairly accurate predictor of default risk, but there have been exceptions. Notably, during the 2007 to 2009 global financial crisis, AAA and Aaa mortgage-backed securities ultimately suffered high default rates.

There are millions of diverse bond issues but only a few bond categories. Most bonds fall into one of these five:

Government bond. This type of bond is a debt security issued by a government to support its spending; it is most often issued in the country's domestic currency. Government debt is money owed by a level of government and is backed by the full faith of the government. Federal government bonds in the United States include (but are not limited to) savings bonds, Treasury bonds, and Treasury inflation-protected securities (TIPS). Before investing in a country's government bonds, investors must assess the inherent risks, including country risk (meaning the soundness—or lack thereof—of a country's economy), political risk, inflation risk, and interest-rate risk.

Agency bond. Agency bonds are issued by institutions originally created by the US government to perform important functions like fostering home ownership and providing student loans. The primary agencies, or *government-sponsored enterprises*, are Fannie Mae, Freddie Mac, and the Student Loan Marketing Association (Sallie Mae). While these agencies technically operate like corporations, they are implicitly backed by the US government.

Municipal bond. Like the US government, state and local governments often borrow money by issuing bonds—just on a smaller scale. Municipal bonds fund an extensive assortment of projects and government functions, ranging from police and fire departments to bridges and toll roads. Municipal bonds are popular among individual investors because they provide tax advantages. Most municipal bonds are free from federal income taxes. This makes municipal bonds especially attractive to investors in high tax brackets. If an investor purchases a municipal bond in the state where he or she resides, it is often free from state and local income taxes as well. Some municipal bonds are *triple tax-free*, which means they are exempt from taxes at the federal, state, and local level.

However, municipal bond investors should be aware that interest received from these bonds may be subject to the individual federal alternative minimum income tax. In addition, interest earned may be taken into account when calculating the taxable portion of an individual's Social Security benefits. The best advice: Always consult a tax advisor before investing in municipal bonds.

Corporate bond. A corporation can issue bonds for many reasons, including expansions, acquisitions, funding stock buybacks, or simply taking advantage of low interest rates. Corporate bonds are almost always taxable at both the federal and state level. As a group, corporate bonds also carry considerably more credit risk than the other types of bonds outlined above. However, the rewards of corporate bonds on a longer-term basis are compelling, a fact that is detailed later in this chapter.

Asset-backed bond. Asset-backed bonds are backed by a pool of underlying debt obligations. This includes residential home mortgages, many of which are directly guaranteed by the federal government (the Government National Mortgage Association, or Ginnie Mae) or through a government agency (Fannie Mae or Freddie Mac). Other asset-backed bonds include *commercial mortgage-backed securities* (CMBSs) and bonds backed by auto or credit card loans (generally called *asset-backed securities*, or ABSs).

A Short History of Bond Yields

According to Treasury bond and Treasury bill return data obtained from the Federal Reserve database in St. Louis, the average ten-year US Treasury bond annualized return since 1928 is 5.23 percent.

But as with stocks, Treasury returns are highly variable. Bond returns are dependent on the starting interest rate and changes in general interest rates over time—that is, when interest rates increase, the value of bonds decreases, and vice versa. This comes into focus if you examine the returns decade by decade.

This fact can have a dramatic impact on future expected returns. Throughout the Great Depression of 1929 to 1933, bond yields declined as economic growth and inflation turned negative. Under the New Deal in the 1930s, the US Treasury issued new bonds at low interest rates to fund public works and America's preparation for and entry into World War II. As a result, yields were soft for the rest of the decade. The ten-year US Treasury yield was at 3.29 percent at the start of 1930 but declined to 2.21 percent by the end of the decade. However, the interest, plus gains in price appreciation, resulted in a total return of 4.48 percent.

During the 1940s, inflation picked up—averaging 6.1 percent—while ten-year Treasury yields averaged only 2.33 percent. The total return during the 1940s was a mere 1.82 percent, well below the average rate of inflation.

In the 1950s, economic growth was modestly strong and interest rates gradually began to climb. By the end of the decade, ten-year US Treasuries were yielding 4.72 percent.

The four decades from 1940 to 1979 were an extended period of rising bond yields, and as discussed earlier, changes in yields have a hefty impact on bond prices. As bond yields first rise in a low-interest rate environment, capital losses become more pronounced, as lower interest payments can only partially offset them. As yields reach higher levels, higher annual coupons, or interest payments, help offset declines in price.

This latter concept became apparent in the 1970s. During that decade, both bond yields and inflation increased dramatically.

Yields on ten-year Treasury bonds increased from 7.79 percent in 1970 to 10.8 percent by 1980, and the annualized return for the decade was an above-average 6.97 percent. However, much of the return earned from interest was offset by declines in price caused by increasing inflation. Inflation averaged 7.8 percent during the ten-year period, making the bonds' *real returns*, or returns after inflation, negative.

In 1981, Federal Reserve Chairman Paul Volcker raised short-term interest rates as high as 20 percent to tame inflation. In the years that followed, inflation and interest rates declined rapidly, pushing up bond prices. The ten-year Treasury yield, which reached a high of 15.8 percent in September 1981, fell as low as 2.05 percent on December 30, 2008. Investors reaped the rewards during this twenty-seven-year period, getting interest alongside capital appreciation from declining bond yields.

The average annual return for ten-year Treasury bonds was 10.36 percent through the 1980s, and during the 1990s, the annualized return was 7.53 percent. In the 2000s, returns matched the long-term average of 5.7 percent.

Most of the long-term returns from bonds over the preceding eighty years came about between 1960 and 2000, when bonds provided a higher-than-average yield component. When you take into consideration the capital appreciation factor caused by declining yields in the 1980s, bonds produced outsized returns for investors for nearly half a century.

Bond yields have continued to decline since 2000, with the ten-year Treasury bond reaching a historic intraday low yield of 1.40 percent in July 2012. Yields have been continually low since that time, and today, the ten-year Treasury bond yields just under 2 percent. Thus after five decades, we have now returned to a similar interest-rate period as the early 1950s.

THE COMPONENTS OF BOND RETURNS

Returns from bonds come from two sources: coupon payments, which are paid out as income, and changes in price. As we witnessed in the discussion on bond history, bond returns were highly variable in each decade. However, over extended periods of time, interest payments ultimately become a much bigger portion of returns than changes in price. For example, more than 90 percent of the total return generated since 1976 from a broadly balanced portfolio of US investment-grade Treasury, agency, and corporate bonds has come from interest payments, not change in price (Table 5.1).

Period Ending 03/31/2013	30 Years	10 Years
Total Return	7.98%	5.03%
Price Return	0.97%	0.57%
Coupon Return (with Reinvestment)	7.88%	4.85%
Other Return (e.g. Paydown)*	-0.20%	-0.32%

Table 5.1: Coupons as a Significant Portion of Bond Returns
Source: Barclays Bank PLC

Brandes Investment Partners reviewed eighty-six years of US and UK equity and fixed-income investment returns, with the results shown in Figure 5.1. The importance of income's contribution to total returns is clear; both stock and bond returns are heavily dependent on the income component. For bonds, it is even more significant.

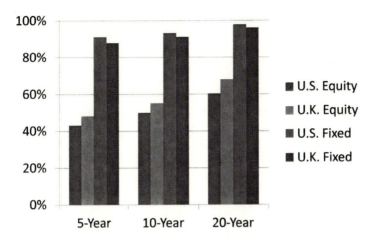

Figure 5.1: Average Income Component of Returns for
Source: Brandes Investment Partners, based on data from Ibbotson
Five-, Ten-, and Twenty-Year Rolling Data
Associates, Global Financial Data, and FactSet, 12/31/2011

SOME FACTS FROM THE BRANDES STUDY:

- Fixed-income, or bond, returns were dominated by the income component for all time horizons longer than five years.

- Over periods of longer than ten years, the income component was dominant over capital appreciation and represented the bulk of returns generated in all income-producing asset classes.

For investors in 2016, there is a negative aspect to this analysis: At the current low levels of interest bonds are generating, it is extremely difficult for traditional buy-and-hold bond investors to generate attractive returns. This is especially true for those investors holding government bonds. In 2016's low-yield environment, clipping coupons on traditional government bonds generates a modest return of less than 2 percent. And this does not account for the fact that interest rates might rise from here, resulting in bond price losses. Unfortunately, interest rates appear likely to stay in this range, given the current modest rates of economic growth.

With interest rates currently at historic lows, the potential return from US Treasury bonds is substantially lower than realized returns from the past several decades. In such an environment, an investor must look beyond traditional government bonds. One attractive class of bonds that pays out higher interest rates are US corporate securities.

THE CORPORATE BOND ADVANTAGE

Unlike government bonds, corporate bonds are subject to credit risk—the probability of, and potential losses that could arise from, a credit event. These could include defaulting on scheduled payments, bankruptcy filing, or restructuring. Corporate bond investors have a wide range of selection in bond maturity lengths, interest rates, credit quality, and provisions.

Corporate bonds are divided into two markets: *investment grade* and *below investment grade* (commonly called *high yield or junk*). Investment-grade corporate bonds carry a relatively low risk of default. As mentioned earlier, rating firms like S&P and Moody's use different designations of upper- and lower-case As, Bs, and Cs to identify a bond's credit quality rating. For example, S&P's medium-quality credit ratings are A and BBB; ratings of BBB and higher are considered investment grade. Credit ratings below these designations (BB, B, CCC, etc.) are considered low credit quality and higher risk—as mentioned before—high yield or junk bonds. The following are some critical features of corporate bonds:

- They are a hybrid security, which indicates that they have a dual nature. They are bonds but can experience equity-like volatility. The value of a corporate bond is closely linked to the issuer's credit quality, its earnings and revenue, and the probability of default.

- They are generally less sensitive to fluctuation in interest rates.

- They have less liquidity in the capital markets, which gives rise to market distortions between the value of bonds and their market price. As uncertainty rises in the markets and the economy, distortion in corporate bond pricing becomes much more likely.

Historically, the promised yield on US corporate bonds rated by S&P as AAA (of the highest quality, issued only by blue-chip companies) has averaged 0.7 percent higher (a figure known as the *credit spread*) than US Treasuries with similar maturities. BBB bonds—the lowest rating given to investment-grade bonds by S&P—have a historical average credit spread of 1.9 percent above Treasuries.

Have investors received these premiums over Treasuries? To answer this question, I examined the long-run evidence in detail. Credit Suisse publishes a book each year that examines the long-term returns of various asset classes, including corporate bonds. US corporate bond data goes as far back as 1900 and the return subset is quite large. Credit Suisse found during the 110-year period from 1900 to 2010, the average annual return of corporate bonds was 2.52 percent per year—0.68 percent per year better than a mix of US Treasury bonds.

Quite a bit of academic research in the past decade has supported favoring corporate bonds over Treasuries. In one study, Alexander Kozhemiakin demonstrated consistently better returns from corporate bonds than Treasuries over time.[25] He also found

---

25 A. Kozhemiakin, "The Risk Premium of Corporate Bonds," The Journal of Portfolio Management, 33(2) (2007): 101–109.

that as investors move to lower-quality bonds, the return differentials become more pronounced. This is especially true in the BB category, where excess returns are the highest of any grade. The lower tier of the investment-grade spectrum—ratings from A/BBB—accounts for two-thirds of the investment-grade market cap and trading activity. Kozhemiakin's findings of higher returns from corporate bonds versus US Treasuries from 1985 to 2005 are shown in Tables 5.2 and 5.3.

Rating	Return	Risk
AAA/AA	8.9%	1.9%
A	9.2%	2.2%
BBB	9.3%	3.3%
BB	11.0%	6.5%
B	9.7%	9.0%
CCC	2.8%	15.2%

Table 5.2: Corporate Bond Historical Returns and Risk,
Source: A. Kozhemiakin, "The Risk Premium of Corporate Bonds,"
January 1985 to December 2005
The Journal of Portfolio Management, 33(2) (2007): 101–109. Risk
measured by annualized standard deviation.

Bonds/Index	5 Years	10 Years	20 Years
BB Rated Bonds	9.29%	8.78%	11.03%
Barclays Aggregate Bond Index	6.52%	5.74%	7.80%
Barclays Govt. Bond Index	5.62%	4.87%	6.76%

Table 5.3: Performance of BB Rated Bonds vs. Bond Index,
Source: A. Kozhemiakin, "The Risk Premium of Corporate Bonds,"
January 1985 to December 2005
The Journal of Portfolio Management, 33(2) (2007): 101–109

Of course, investors *should* expect corporate bonds to trade at higher yields than US Treasury bonds over extended periods of time. As I mentioned, the primary difference between the two yields is known as the credit spread, but credit risk is not the only factor that leads corporate bonds to deliver better returns than government bonds. Other key factors include tax treatment, illiquidity, call features, and the unique provisions that are included in the contracts of corporate bonds—characteristics that government bonds simply don't offer.

Most investors believe that corporate bonds' higher returns are strictly due to their credit risk, but academic research has concluded otherwise. For example, Jing-zhi Huang of Penn State University and Ming Huang of Stanford University found that less than a third of the excess return from investment-grade bonds is associated with default risk.[26] Gordon Delianedis and Robert Geske of UCLA's Anderson School found that among AAA-rated firms, only a small fraction (5 percent) of the excess returns provided were attributable to default risk. Furthermore, they determined that among BBB-rated firms, which are rated just above junk, only 22 percent of the credit spread can be attributed to default risk.[27] Ultimately, Delianedis and Geske concluded that credit risk and credit spreads above government bonds cannot solely be correlated to the possibility of default, leverage, or a firm's specific risk. Instead, they are primarily attributable to tax consequences, liquidity, and market risk factors.[28]

But are the results of these academic studies consistent with actual default rates? According to Credit Suisse, default rates for all rated corporate bond issuers since 1900 has averaged 1.14 percent per year, while riskier high-yield bonds averaged 2.84 percent.[29] Of course,

---

26 Jing-zhi Huang and Ming Huang, "How Much of the Corporate–Treasury Yield Spread Is Due to Credit Risk?" Stanford University Working Paper, 2002, No. FIN-02-04.

27 Robert L. Geske and Gordon Delianedis, "The Components of Corporate Credit Spreads: Default, Recovery, Taxes, Jumps, Liquidity, and Market Factors," UCLA Anderson Working Paper, 2001, No. 22-01.

28 Ibid.

29 Credit Suisse Global Investment Returns Yearbook, 2016.

during chaotic economic periods, the default rate has reached much higher extremes. Default rates for investment-grade bonds peaked at 8.45 percent in 1933, during the Great Depression; in the same year, speculative bonds had a default rate of 15.48 percent. According to default data and yearly results maintained by S&P, the default rate for all investment-grade corporate bonds (those rated above BB) has averaged below 1 percent since 2001 (Table 5.4).

Year	Investment-Grade Defaults (#)	Investment-Grade Default Rate (%)
2001	6	0.33
2002	10	0.56
2003	0	0
2004	1	0.06
2005	1	0.06
2006	0	0
2007	0	0
2008	11	0.73
2009	5	0.34
2010	0	0
2011	1	0.07
2012	0	0

Table 5.4: US Investment-Grade Corporate Bond Default Summary Sources: S&P's Global Fixed Income Research and S&P's Credit Pro.

When you consider the low default rates of the 2000s, the long-run return premium of 0.68 percent per year for the highest grade, AAA, seems puzzlingly high. No AAA or AA+ corporate bond has defaulted since 1991, so that is a very eye-catching return premium. A 3 percent-plus premium for BB bonds seems downright generous, given the fact that the annual default rate for these bonds during the financial collapse of 2008 was below 3 percent and, according to S&P, their average default rate has been below 1 percent per year since 1981 (Table 5.5).

Year	BBB+	BBB+	BBB-	BB+	BB	BB-
1981	0	0	0	0	0	0
1982	0	0.69	0	0	2.86	7.14
1983	0	0	1.35	2.27	0	1.64
1984	0	1.41	0	0	1.72	1.56
1985	0	0	0	1.69	1.56	1.39
1986	0	0.78	0	1.85	1.22	1.14
1987	0	0	0	0	0	0.83
1988	0	0	0	0	0	2.34
1989	0.91	0.81	0	0	0	2
1990	0.77	0	1.11	1.43	3.09	4.5
1991	0.84	0.76	0	3.77	1.14	1.05
1992	0	0	0	0	0	0
1993	0	0	0	0	1.96	0
1994	0	0	0	0	0.89	0
1995	0	0	0.72	0	1.67	1.23
1996	0	0	0	0.98	0	0.62
1997	0.48	0	0	0	0	0.47
1998	0	0.36	0	0	0.71	0.45
1999	0	0.38	0.45	0.85	1.31	0.81
2000	0	0.37	0.91	0	1.26	3.33
2001	0.41	0.71	0.44	0.83	1.3	4.62
2002	1.21	0.69	2.14	1.82	1.17	4.02
2003	0	0	0	0.9	1.6	0.4
2004	0	0	0	0	1.18	0.39
2005	0	0.3	0	0.8	0	0.4
2006	0	0	0	0.87	0	0.41
2007	0	0	0	0	0.54	0.39
2008	0.45	0.76	0.93	2.52	0.63	0.78
2009	0.49	0.37	0.86	0	1.43	0.89
2010	0	0	0	0	0	0
2011	0	0	0.39	0	0	0
2012	0	0	0	0	0	0
	BBB+	BBB+	BBB-	BB+	BB	BB-
Average	0.17	0.26	0.29	0.64	0.85	1.34

Stand. Dev.	0.33	0.37	0.52	0.96	0.87	1.68
Minimum	0	0	0	0	0	0
Maximum	1.21	1.41	2.14	3.77	3.09	7.14

Table 5.5: US Corporate Default Rates, Bonds Rated BB- to BBB+
Sources: S&P's Global Fixed Income Research
and S&P's Credit Pro.

Researchers have also concluded that actual default rates are much lower than ratings might suggest. Stephen Kealhofer, Sherry Kwok, and Wenlong Weng found true default rates for AAA bonds of 0.13 percent, while the riskier BB rating category had a default rate of only 1.42 percent.[30] As reported by S&P, the actual rate since 1981 is below 1 percent for BB+ and BB bonds, and BB-rated bonds had a default rate slightly above 1 percent (Table 5.6).

	BBB+	BBB+	BBB-	BB+	BB	BB-
Average Default Rate, 1981–2012	0.17	0.26	0.29	0.64	0.85	1.34

Table 5.6: Average Default Rate, Bonds Rated BB- to BBB+
Source: "Uses and Abuses of Bond Default Rates." Stephen Kealhofer,
Sherry Kwok, and Wenlong Weng. Document Number: 999-0000-039.

This indicates that the default line between BBB- and BB-rated bonds is very thin. Given that the actual risk of default is historically quite low, it seems likely that other factors are at work, such as their illiquidity. An illiquid asset cannot be sold easily without a noticeable loss in value or quickly because of a lack of ready-and-willing buyers. Lower-rated corporate bonds have a larger-than-normal discrepancy between the asking prices of sellers and the bidding prices of buyers because there is low demand for them. Thus, the illiquidity of corporate bonds has a larger-than-expected effect on their returns.

---

30 Stephen Kealhofer, Sherry Kwok, and Wenlong Weng, "Uses and Abuses of Bond Default Rates," Document Number: 999-0000-039.

Since volume of transactions for corporate bonds is far below that of government bonds and increased liquidity is an attractive quality for any investment, investors demand extra remuneration for holding securities that are less liquid and thus more expensive to sell.

For corporate bonds, this *illiquidity premium* shows up in higher interest-rate spreads over otherwise comparable government securities. So says the theory of several prominent researchers, including Patrick Houweling, Albert Mentink, and Ton Vorst. In a 2005 article, they analyzed the effect of liquidity risk on corporate bond credit spreads based on a sample of 999 investment-grade corporate bonds.[31] In the paper, they controlled two common factors: 1) excess returns from the stock market and 2) excess returns from long-term corporate bonds over long-term Treasury bonds, in addition to the rating and maturity of each bond. Houweling et al found that liquidity risk explains a significant portion of observed credit risk spreads.

Corporate bonds also carry a substantial amount of volatility risk. Although their actual default risk is below expectations, recessions have the power to drive them to default. While relatively safe during most economic periods, corporate bonds become a far riskier asset in recessionary periods, perhaps most notably demonstrated during the Great Recession of 2008 and 2009. As a result, some pundits argue that the corporate bond asset class is less appropriate for long-term investors who hold a substantial portion of equity in their portfolios, because other fixed-income asset classes (namely, government bonds) do a better job of reducing risk. In 2008, an investor who held Treasury bonds instead of corporate bonds would have had substantially less portfolio volatility. On the other hand, in the very next year corporate bonds rebounded strongly.

---

31 Patrick Houweling, Albert Mentink, and Ton Vorst, "Comparing Possible Proxies of Corporate Bond Liquidity," *Journal of Banking and Finance*, 29 (2005): 1,331–1,358.

If you can tolerate the inherent volatility of corporate bonds—especially during recessions—you should strongly consider them as a long-term investment option. Investors who concentrate their corporate bond holdings in the BBB and BB ratings universe reap particularly good benefits. These bonds have the potential to reward investors with a 3 percent annualized premium over a government bond of a similar duration.

Trading individual corporate bonds is quite different from trading stocks. Stocks can be bought at uniform prices and are traded through exchanges, but most bonds trade over the counter, priced by individual brokers. However, in the last decade, price transparency has improved. In 1999, the Bond Price Competition Improvement Act of 1999 placed new rules on clarity and candor in bond pricing. In response to the law's requirements, the Securities Industry and Financial Markets Association created the site Investinginbonds. com. There, investors can see current prices for bonds that have traded more than four times in the preceding day. Thanks to the law and the subsequent availability of real-time reporting of many bond trades, investors are better off than they once were.

Many well-regarded brokerages, including Charles Schwab, TD Ameritrade, and Fidelity Investments, now have websites devoted to bond pricing and trading. Fidelity discloses its fee structure for all corporate bonds, making it clear what it will cost you per bond—$1. Other online brokers charge flat fees, regardless of the number of bonds traded. Depending on the number of bonds you plan to trade, one broker may be more advantageous than another.

On the secondary market, there are spreads between the buy and sell prices. Keep in mind that trading-fee disclosures do not divulge the spreads between the buy and sell prices embedded in the transaction. You must comparison shop in order to find the best transaction price after all fees are taken into account. Some sites charge no transaction fees at all and instead embed their fees in the spread.

Corporate bond price spreads may be high or low, depending on the issuer. In many instances, the *bid* (the price at which you sell) is 75 to 150 basis points (0.75 percent to 1.5 percent) below the *ask* (the price at which you buy).

Despite the inherent complications of bond pricing and a lack of transparency, investing in individual corporate bonds can offer significant rewards. First, they give investors the luxury of knowing exactly how much they will receive in interest each year. In addition, the individual investment is protected against interest-rate risk, but only over the full term of the bond.

When interest rates are at historic lows, any long-term investment strategy should take the potential yield effect into consideration. Since the largest portion of return for an investor will come in the form of income, it's paramount to seek out higher-income alternatives, especially since higher-yielding bonds are less sensitive to interest-rate fluctuations. From 1996 to 2012, higher-yielding bonds have traded at a wide range of prices.

In Figure 5.2, the coupon (or yield) is shown versus the price change. In some years, like 2008, high-yield bonds' prices dropped dramatically versus the income collected; the reverse was true in 2009. However, the total return graph shows that despite the price moves over time, the overall return for higher yielding bonds primarily came from their coupons. The average annualized coupon over the time period shown is 9 percent.

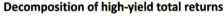

Decomposition of high-yield total returns

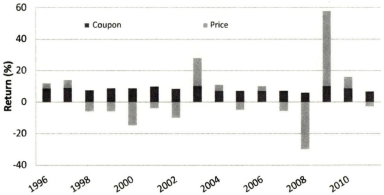

Figure 5.2: Decomposition of High-Yield Returns,
Sources: TIAA-CREF, Bank of America Merrill Lynch, and
Bloomberg, 2012. January 1996 to December 2011

Higher-yielding bonds are also much less sensitive to high interest rates—mostly because economic conditions are generally good when interest rates rise. In a strong economic environment, the default rate usually drops, and lower default rates make higher-yielding bonds a more attractive investment. Higher-yielding bonds also offer investors more annual income, which reduces the bond's sensitivity to changes in interest rates.

Period Range	10-Year Treasury Starting Yield	10-Year Treasury Change in Yield	Total Return Over Period
09/30/1998–01/31/2000	4.42%	2.25	3.97%
10/31/2001–12/31/2001	4.27%	0.77	2.52%
02/28/2002–03/31/2002	4.87%	0.55	2.38%
09/30/2002–11/30/2002	3.61%	0.61	5.10%
05/31/2003–08/31/2003	3.35%	1.1	2.58%
03/31/2004–06/30/2004	3.84%	0.78	-0.88%
08/31/2005–10/31/2005	4.02%	0.54	-1.71%
12/31/2005–06/30/2006	4.40%	0.74	3.01%
03/31/2008–06/30/2008	3.43%	0.55	1.80%

12/31/2008–02/28/2009	2.25%	0.79	1.80%
03/31/2009–06/30/2009	2.69%	0.84	22.55%
11/30/2009–12/31/2009	3.20%	0.83	3.00%
08/31/2010–03/31/2011	2.48%	0.97	10.08%
Average	**3.60%**	**0.86**	**4.32%**

Table 5.7: High-Yield Bonds' Sensitivity to Higher Interest Rates
Sources: TIAA-CREF, Bank of America Merrill
Lynch, and Bloomberg, 2012. Interest Rates

Reinvestment of bond income can have a powerful effect. As shown in Figure 5.3, a $10,000 investment in a 20-year corporate bond paying 5 percent interest (the prevailing rate for BBB investment-grade corporate bonds) would provide $10,000 in income over the life of the bond. Reinvesting the interest earned at the same 5 percent rate, however, increases the value of the gain by more than half, from $10,000 to $16,850.64. Thus, the value of the investment over the twenty-year period would increase to $26,850.64, rather than the $20,000 total of principal and interest collected over time without reinvestment.

*Assumes income reinvested semiannually at 5%. Numbers Rounded.

Figure 5.3: The Power of Compounding Bond Interest
Sources: TIAA-CREF, Bank of America Merrill Lynch, and Bloomberg, 2012.

As mentioned previously, time is an investor's greatest ally. The negative effects of volatility are reduced over time, so a longer time horizon can afford you greater flexibility in constructing a bond portfolio. Above all, time empowers the snowball effect of reinvesting bond interest to work for you.

Total Return Investing with Pepsi Bonds

Consider this example: A corporate bond issued by Pepsi in May, 1998 carried a 6.5 percent coupon with a maturity of 15 years. Interest rates were on the rise from 1988 to 2000, as measured by the ten-year US Treasury bond rates' climb from 5.6 percent to 6.45 percent between May 1998 and January 2000.

Suppose an investor wanted to purchase Pepsi corporate bonds at the end of 1999— one hundred Pepsi bonds, specifically, each with a par value of $1,000. On December 31, 2000, she could purchase the bonds at a discount from par for approximately $919 per bond—thus costing her $91,900 for one hundred bonds. If the investor decided to keep her investment total at $100,000, she could buy 108, rather than one hundred, Pepsi bonds. Those 108 bonds would produce an initial income of $7,020 per year.

Date	Bonds Held	Bond Price	Coupon	Interest Payout	Bonds Repurchased	Value + Cash Remainder
12/31/1999	100	—	—	—	—	—
12/31/2000	108	$1,026.00	6.50%	$7,020.00	8.00	$118,576.00
12/31/2001	116	$1,013.00	6.50%	$7,540.00	7.00	$123,888.00
12/31/2002	123	$1,075.00	6.50%	$7,930.00	7.00	$138,714.00
12/31/2003	130	$1,069.00	6.50%	$8,385.00	8.00	$146,286.00
12/31/2004	138	$1,062.00	6.50%	$8,905.00	9.00	$154,399.00
12/30/2005	147	$1,043.00	6.50%	$9,490.00	9.00	$161,768.00
12/29/2006	156	$1,070.00	6.50%	$10,075.00	9.00	$175,925.00
12/31/2007	166	$1,090.00	6.50%	$10,660.00	10.00	$189,420.00
12/31/2008	176	$1,031.00	6.50%	$11,310.00	10.00	$190,704.00
12/31/2009	186	$1,027.00	6.50%	$11,960.00	13.00	$200,928.00
12/31/2010	198	$1,023.00	6.50%	$12,805.00	12.00	$214,336.00

12/30/2011	210	$1,014.00	6.50%	$13,585.00	13.00	$225,511.00
12/31/2012	224	$1,010.00	6.50%	$14,430.00	15.00	$238,650.00
05/31/2013	224	Maturity + final interest payment				

Table 5.8: Pepsi Bond Example
Source: Bloomberg

Each year, she could choose to reinvest her interest proceeds and buy additional Pepsi bonds at the prevailing market price (Table 5.8). By 2012, only thirteen years after her original investment of $100,000, the investor now has $253,080—a 7.4 percent annualized return. This return was primarily accrued through interest—more than $145,000. Table 5.9 shows a synopsis of Pepsi bond prices at the end of each year, along with the prevailing government bond interest rates and the duration of the Pepsi bonds.

What Is Duration?

The term *duration* has a unique meaning in the context of bonds. It is a measurement of how long (in terms of years) it will take for a bond's cost to be repaid by its internal cash flows. Duration is a vital consideration for investors, as bonds with higher durations carry more risk and have higher price volatility than those with lower durations.

Date	10-Year US Treasury Yield	Pepsi Bond Duration	Pepsi Bond Price
12/31/2000	6.4	9.6	$1,026.00
12/31/2001	5.1	8.2	$1,013.00
12/31/2002	4	7.7	$1,075.00
12/31/2003	4.2	7.2	$1,069.00
12/31/2004	4.3	6.6	$1,062.00
12/30/2005	4.4	5.9	$1,043.00
12/29/2006	4.7	5.3	$1,070.00
12/31/2007	3.9	4.5	$1,090.00
12/31/2008	2.2	3.7	$1,031.00
12/31/2009	3.8	2.9	$1,027.00
12/31/2010	3.3	2.2	$1,023.00
12/30/2011	1.9	1.3	$1,014.00
12/31/2012	1.9	0.4	$1,010.00

Table 5.9: Pepsi Bond Analysis Table
Source: Bloomberg

A few closing notes to ponder as you consider the Pepsi bond example:

- Reinvesting bond interest is *just as important* as reinvesting stock dividends. The same facts you saw in the example of Pepsi stock analysis are true here: The more bonds you own, the more interest you will collect each year.

- Reinvestment in individual bonds is generally best for investors who have larger portfolios and plenty of time to closely analyze the securities before they buy them. Bond mutual funds are more appropriate for investors with smaller accounts.

- I have listed below 50 corporate bonds that are available to investors primarily in the BBB and BB S&P rated categories.

1-25	26-50
Gap Inc. 5.95% 4/12/2021	Telecom Italia 7.175% 6/18/2019
Arcelormittal Luxembourg 6.25% 8/5/2020	Sara Lee Corp. 6.125% 11/01/2032
Newmont Mining 3.5% 3/15/2022	Pulte Group 6.375% 5/15/2033
KLA-Tencor 4.65% 11/1/2024	Newfield Exploration 5.75% 1/30/2022
Ensco PLC 4.5% 10/01/2024	Neiman Marcus Group Inc. 7.125% 6/1/2028
Coach Inc. 4.25% 4/1/25	Humana Inc. 6.3% 8/1/2018
Suntrust Bank 6% 2/15/2026	HCA Inc. 7.5% 2/15/2022
Expedia Inc. 4.5% 8/15/2024	Wyndham Worldwide 3.9% 3/1/2023
Wendy's 7.0% 12/15/2025	Morgan Stanley 5.5% 7/28/2021
Royal Caribbean Cruises 7.5% 10/15/2027	Tyson Foods Inc. 3.95% 8/15/2024
Goldman Sachs Group 5.95% 1/15/2027	Liberty Media Corp. 8.5% 7/15/2029
Petrobras Int'l 5.375% 1/27/2021	R. R. Donnelley & Sons 6.125% 1/15/2017
Southwest Airlines 5.125% 3/1/2017	Amerada Hess Corp. 7.3% 8/15/2031
Alcoa Inc. 5.125% 10/01/2024	Kohls Corp. 6% 1/15/2033
Nokia Corp. 5.375% 5/15/2019	Regions Financial Corp. 7.375% 12/10/2037
Toll Bros. 5.875% 2/15/2022	Valero Energy Corp. 6.125% 6/15/2017
Constellation Brands Inc. 4.25% 5/1/2023	Ford Motor Co. 6.5% 8/1/2018
Hertz Corp. 7% 1/15/2028	Health Care Reit Inc. 5.25% 1/15/2022
Masco Corp. 7.1255 3/15/2020	CBS Corp. 3.5% 1/15/2025
Safeway Inc. 7.45% 9/15/2027	Juniper Networks Inc. 4.35% 6/15/2025
Hartford Financial 5.5% 3/30/2020	L-3 Communications Corp. 4.95% 2/15/2021
Devon Energy Corp. 5.85% 12/15/2025	Laboratory Corp. 4% 11/01/2023
Limited Brands Inc. 6.95% 3/1/2033	Nasdaq Inc. 4.25% 6/1/2024
Sunoco Inc. 5.75% 1/15/2017	Quest Diagnostics Inc. 4.25% 4/1/2024
Seacor Holdings Inc. 7.375% 10/01/2019	Zions Bancorp. 4.5% 6/13/2023

Table 5.10: 50 Corporate Bonds
Source: Bondsonline.com

- If you have a large enough portfolio to invest in individual bonds, I strongly suggest you utilize a bond ladder. A bond ladder is a portfolio of bonds in which each security has a significantly diverse maturity date. The primary rationale of purchasing a number of smaller bonds with different maturity dates rather than one large bond with a single maturity date is to minimize interest-rate risk and to increase liquidity. Interest payments from the bonds in a ladder can offer on schedule cash flows. In addition, the ladder can help you deal with reinvestment risk. For example, if an investor would put all its fixed income dollars into a single corporate bond, the bond would eventually mature. There is uncertainty at that point in time at what interest rates will be. Thus you could be stuck reinvesting all your money appropriated for fixed income at a lower interest rate. This is what is known as reinvestment risk. Building a bond ladder has the potential to spread this reinvestment risk across a number of bonds that mature at different time intervals. Imagine that interest rates fall as one of your short term bonds in the ladder approaches maturity. If you choose to reinvest, you will have to invest only a fraction of your overall bond portfolio at the lower rate. Meanwhile, the other bonds in the portfolio will continue generating income at the higher older interest rates. So any impact on your income from a corporate bond during periods of falling interest rates will be smaller with a bond ladder than with a single purchase and single maturity.

- What if instead interest rates rise? Maintaining a bond ladder is also a positive for an investor in this case. An investor can take advantage of the higher interest rates when one of the bonds in the portfolio matures. A bond ladder also takes out the risk of a single bond issuer defaulting and ruining your principal. Overall, a bond ladder is a strong risk reduction element in maintaining a portfolio of corporate bonds.

CHAPTER 6

THE COVERED-CALL STRATEGY

"Only a fool holds out for top dollar."

—Joseph P. Kennedy, 1888–1969

A s I'VE DESCRIBED in the preceding chapters, a snowball approach to stock investing allows you to focus not on the *price* of the shares you own, but instead on how *many* shares you own. The paramount element to true wealth building is accumulating additional shares of stock through reinvestment of dividends paid, as that allows your stocks' value to grow even when the markets are simply treading water (about half the time). Now that you know that, it's time to learn about options, and specifically about the benefits of the *covered-call strategy*.

> ## A Short Glossary of Option Terms
>
> **Call option:** A contract that grants its owner the right, but not the obligation, to buy one hundred shares of a specific stock by or before a specific date and at a specific fixed price.

Call owner: The individual who owns the call option.

Call writer: The individual who sells the call option.

Call away: The practice of buying one hundred shares of stock in a call option.

Underlying security: The stock or other type of security the option contract is written for; it cannot be exchanged or replaced.

Exercise: Using a call option to trade in the underlying security. Exercising an option means that the call owner can *call away* (buy) one hundred shares of stock.

Strike price: The specific price per share at which one hundred shares of stock can be bought or sold when a call option is exercised.

Expiration cycle: The months in which call options expire. There are three annual cycles known by the following acronyms: JAJO (January, April, July, October); FMAN (February, May, August, November); and MJSD (March, June, September, December).

Expiration date: The date on which an option expires and becomes worthless.

Premium: The current value of an option, which is the amount a call-option buyer has to pay to the call-option seller to acquire the option, or the amount the call-option seller receives from the call-option buyer.

Time value: The portion of an option premium that is based on the time remaining until the call option's expiration; as the expiration date approaches, time value declines at an accelerated pace.

Uncovered call: An option contract sold by an investor who does not own one hundred shares of the underlying security.

Covered-call strategy: The practice of selling one call per one hundred shares owned of the underlying stock. If exercised, market risk is eliminated because shares are available to be called away. Covered-call writers receive the premium and earn dividends as long as they own the stock.

Forward roll: Roll forward is to extend the expiration or maturity of an option or futures contract by closing the initial shorter-term contract and opening a new longer-term contract for the same underlying asset

If you add a covered-call strategy to your investment mix, you can add even more income to what you're already receiving as a dividend-yielding stockholder. A covered-call strategy involves selling or writing *call options* against a held position in an *underlying security*, which is known as *covered-call writing*. Investors write covered calls primarily for the following two reasons:

- to realize a supplementary return on a stock position by earning *premium* income

- for protection against a decline in the stock's price

Covered-call writing is considered the most conservative strategy in option writing. While it remains unknown to most investors, it is in fact safer than outright stock ownership because the investor's downside risk is offset by premium income received for selling the *call provision*. Covered-call writing can either be accomplished by the sale of a call option against a stock you currently hold or through the simultaneous purchase of a stock and the sale of a call option.

One call option is sold for every one hundred shares of stock held. As a *call writer*, you will receive cash for selling a call, but you will be compelled to sell the stock at the *strike price* of the call if the stock is assigned out of your account. In effect, an investor with a covered-call strategy is compensated with a premium for agreeing to sell his or her holdings at the strike price. In exchange for being paid this premium, the investor relinquishes any increase in the stock's price above the set strike price to the *call owner*. A call option also has an *expiration date*, which is the date on which the option expires and becomes worthless. The call owner has the right to exercise the contract and thus call away, or buy, the call writer's shares. Thus, call buyers assume broad risk.

According to the Options Clearing Corporation's latest (2014) results,[32] less than 20 percent of all option contracts that were opened ended up being exercised. Thus, a call buyer is practicing a highly speculative strategy. Most traders use options to time their entry and exit points into a stock in order to benefit from short-term price movements. But prices substantially decline as expiration nears, so in most cases, options lose their value dramatically and are infrequently exercised.

The chief argument against a covered-call strategy is that if the stock's price rises above the call option's strike price, the stock's potential profits narrow to the price specified in the *indenture*. However, if you believe that a stock's price has exceeded its normalized historical valuation based on its dividend yield analysis (more on this below), writing covered calls against the position can be a sagacious methodology to generate additional income.

---

32 Options Clearing Corporation, "TradeKing Options Playbook," https://investor.tradeking.com/PrivateView/edu/opb/opbCashingOutYourOptions.tmpl.

Examples of Covered Calls

The first rule of covered-call writing is this: Pick a company that you already own whose current stock price, you believe, is above your target price and whose dividend yield has fallen below its historical averages. We'll revisit Pepsi (PEP) and Northern Trust (NTRS) as the companies used in these examples.

Consider an investor who already owns one hundred Pepsi shares, which were purchased in September 2011 at a price of $65 per share. At the same time, the investor also purchased one hundred Northern Trust shares for $35 per share. PEP closed at $97.20 and yielded a dividend of 3.1 percent, and NTRS closed at $67.18 and yielded a dividend of 2.2 percent on January 7, 2016. Since both stocks have risen by a substantial amount since their purchase, the investor wants to protect his positions in the stock without selling and at the same time potentially acquire additional income.

His first step is to select the best strike price. All the strike prices shown in Table 6.1 are slightly above the stocks' current trading price, but the premium levels are quite different. As you can see in Tables 6.1 and 6.2, the more time remains before the call option's expiration, the higher the value will be for the call closest to the stock's current price. The closer the strike price is to the current price of the stock, the higher the premium will be.

To help make the decision process easier on which calls to sell, annualize the returns of these options for the sake of comparison. An investor can calculate a yield by dividing the option premium by the current stock price. Then, divide the yield by the number of months in the holding period and multiply by 12 (the number of months in a year). The total is the calculated yield that would be earned if the position were kept open for a full year (Table 6.2).

Stock	Strike Price ($)	Premium ($)	
		April Expiration	July Expiration
PEP	100	1.94	3.15
	105	0.61	1.55
	110	0.18	0.60
NTRS	70	1.87	3.26
	75	0.70	1.55
	80	0.20	0.80

Table 6.1: Option Values for PEP and NTRS
Source: Yahoo Finance

Stock	Strike Price ($)	Premium ($)	
		April (3 Months)	July (3 Months)
PEP	100	$(1.94 \div 99.20) \div 3 \times 12$ = 5.43 percent	$(3.15 \div 99.20) \div 6 \times 12 =$ 4.41 percent
	105	$(0.61 \div 99.20) \div 3 \times 12$ = 1.73 percent	$(1.55 \div 99.20) \div 6 \times 12 =$ 2.18 percent
	110	$(0.18 \div 99.20) \div 3 \times 12$ = 0.51 percent	$(0.60 \div 99.20) \div 6 \times 12 =$ 0.86 percent
NTRS	70	$(1.87 \div 67.18) \div 3 \times 12$ = 7.73 percent	$(3.26 \div 67.18) \div 6 \times 12 =$ 6.73 percent
	75	$(0.70 \div 67.18) \div 3 \times 12 =$ 2.89 percent	$(1.55 \div 67.18) \div 6 \times 12 =$ 3.10 percent
	80	$(0.20 \div 67.18) \div 3 \times 12 =$ 0.82 percent	$(0.80 \div 67.18) \div 6 \times 12 =$ 1.65 percent

Table 6.2: Calculating Annualized Yield for PEP and NTRS Options
Source: Yahoo Finance

The Four Possible Outcomes from Writing Pepsi Covered Calls @ $105 Strike Price

1. *The call option expires and you keep the proceeds.* Pepsi stock never reaches the strike price. In this event, the premium you received is 100 percent profit. In the example shown in Table 6.1, if you sold a covered call against the $105

strike price in Pepsi for April, you would collect a $0.61 premium for each share you owned, or $61 for one hundred shares. You would also have collected the quarterly dividend of $0.7025 per share ($70.25) along the way.

2. *You close the position to secure a profit or to limit a loss.* You are free to close a call option that you wrote any time before it expires. If the call's premium drops substantially, it might make sense to take your profits. You can then take the proceeds and always write calls that are above the current price and expire at a later point in time.

3. *The covered call is exercised.* This can happen at any time, but it most commonly occurs on the last trading day of the month of expiration. In the case of exercise on the last day, your one hundred shares are called away and your net profits include the premium you received on selling the call provision ($61) along with the quarterly dividend of $70.25. Since the strike price was $105, you would also collect the gains from the point you wrote the call ($105-$99.20). The downside is anything above the $105 price point in share price gain you would have sacrificed.

4. *You roll forward your covered call.* Covered-call writers can avoid an exercise by closing the call and replacing it with one that expires later. The *forward roll* works because a later-expiring contract is always worth more, since it has a longer period of time before it expires. Make sure to avoid the transaction becoming "unqualified". Ensure you write a call or roll forward a call against your stock with a strike price greater than or equal to the previous day's closing price and with 30 or more days till expiration. Thus, there will be no effect on the holding period of your stock.

Annualized returns are a solid gauge to value and compare

two firms for covered-call writing. There are always a multitude of factors that ultimately determine annualized yield. These include daily movement in a stock's price, changes in markets, dividend payments, and timing between entry date and expiration of an option. When a snowball investor is picking a covered-call strategy, a strong consideration should be placed upon dividend yield in addition to premium income on an annualized basis. Remember, the covered call writer earns any dividends paid on the call-covered stock until it is called. Pepsi currently yields 2.8 percent, higher than Northern Trust's 2.2 percent. Pepsi's ex-dividend date is March 3, 2016, and Northern Trust's is one day earlier, March 2, 2016. If the stocks had different ex-dividend dates, the premium pricing would also be affected as well as the potential for the option to be exercised.

Covered writing does invite some risk. For example if Pepsi's stock price fell to $90, the loss on the stock position ($99.20 − $90.00 = $9.20) would surpass the sum of the dividends and call sale proceeds ($0.61 + $0.7025 = $1.31). It would have been much better for a trader to actually sell Pepsi at that point in time. Alternatively, the price of the stock could well exceed $105. In this case the investor might lament the writing of the call. However, a snowball investor is not concerned as much with the price of the actual stock, but the income they receive. If Pepsi stock does drop to $90, a snowball investor can simply buy more shares as the stock will be more attractive from a payout perspective.

Not every shareholder holding one hundred shares of a stock should sell covered calls. In some cases, you're better off selling your shares, taking the profits, and buying another dividend-bearing stock that offers a higher yield and more potential. One way to prevent call writing regret is to write a call only when your stock is highly overvalued on a dividend yield basis. For example, you would write a call on Pepsi shares only when the dividend yield dropped to the lowest end of the historical range (2.25%-2.5%) based upon the strike price. In my example above, if Pepsi traded to the strike price of $105 per share, its dividend yield would be ($2.81/$105.00) or 2.6%. A better option might be to wait for Pepsi shares to trade above that level and then sell a covered call. If Pepsi stock continued to advance in 2016 to $115 a share, you could then sell a covered call at $120 a share. At $120 a share, Pepsi's dividend yield would 2.34% ($2.81/$120.00). You could then easily feel comfortable that if Pepsi advances and your shares are called, you ended up liquidating your position in Pepsi at the $120 strike price and at the lowest historical yield point.

Another item to consider is the potential tax consequences? Income from a covered call is always treated as a short-term capital gain or rolled into the capital gain on exercised stock. There's also the risk of a more serious tax consequence: possibly losing the benefit of long-term gain treatment. If you sell a call that is lower than one increment from its latest closing price in most cases (meaning the strike is well below the stock's current market value), you could be required to treat the gain as a short-term profit.

Final Guidelines for Writing Covered Calls

- Never buy a stock just to write a covered call. Apply a sensible standard: Pick companies whose stock you want to own because of their higher than average dividend growth.

- Be willing to accept exercise when it happens. When you sell a covered call, you are granting someone the right to call away your stock. You need to be prepared to sell your one hundred shares for the strike price at any point in time after you write the covered call. Have a replacement stock picked out so your funds will not sit idle and will still be able to earn competitive dividends.

- Pick a strike price higher than the price you paid for the stock and at a point where the historical yield for the stock is at its lowest point. I never recommend writing covered calls with strikes below the current price—they are much more likely to get exercised.

- Most critically, include dividend income when making your comparison. When you are comparing potential income from covered calls, always remember that dividends do play a role in the overall return. If the fundamentals are approximately equal on two or more stocks you are considering writing covered calls against, opt for the company with a lower dividend yield or the company with a dividend payment farther in the future. Make sure you're not sacrificing income, as the income component is the most critical factor of long-term wealth building.

CHAPTER 7

THE FUTURE AND THE TOP 100

"The further backward you look, the further ahead you can see."

—Winston Churchill, 1874–1965

N ow you know the truth—investments that generate income were the key to earning consistent returns
throughout the last one hundred and ten years. Here's
the bad news: Today, the income component from both stocks and
bonds are near cycle lows. As recently as 1990, Dow stocks provided a healthy average dividend yield of over 4 percent; in fact,
the average dividend yield had hovered around the 4 percent mark
since 1906. More importantly, that 4 percent has contributed
nearly half of all stock appreciation for more than a decade. This
is not just the case for the 30 firms within the Dow. Vanguard
Total Stock Market ETF, which tracks approximately 100% of the
investable U.S. stock market and includes large-, mid-, small-, and
micro-cap stocks regularly traded on the New York Stock Exchange
and Nasdaq, yields an anemic 1.9%

Tables 7.1 and 7.2 below show the average dividend yield for
the Dow since 1906 by year and by decade, respectively. In the

fifty years following the 1906 San Francisco earthquake, dividends were considered the most important consideration for owning stocks, but the average dividend yield of the stock market has slowly eroded over time.

The current cash dividend on the 1,000 largest US companies represents a mere 32 percent of reported earnings (payout ratio) —well below the high points of the last fifty years. According to longrundata.com, the historical highs in dividend payout ratios occurred in 1960 (63.8 percent) and 1991 (67.2 percent).[33] The dividend payout ratio is the percentage of earnings (aka net income or the "bottom line") a firm pays its shareholders in the form of dividends. Pepsi expects net income of $4.70 per share in earnings this year, and the firm will pay out $2.81 in dividends to its shareholders. This indicates the company has a payout ratio of 59 percent—nearly double today's payout ratio for the average US company. Today's extremely low dividend yields are a direct outcome not only of the lower payout ratio, but also the fantastic rise in stock prices during the bull market of the 1990s.

For investors to get back to the 1991 average yield of 4 percent, US firms would have to double their payout ratios, or stock prices would have to tumble much lower. This occurred in March 2009, when the Dow dropped to its lowest point in recent history, 6,547. The average yield on Dow stocks at that point in time was 3.8 percent.

---

33 *Ibbotson SBBI 2015 Classic Yearbook: Market Results for Stocks, Bonds, Bills, and Inflation*, Morningstar: Chicago (2015).

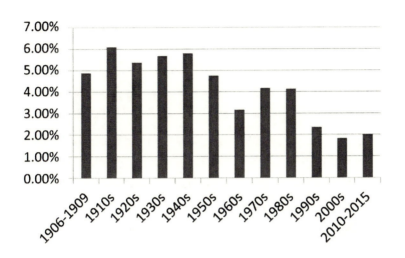

Figure 7.1: Average Dow Dividend Yield by Decade from 1906 to 2015

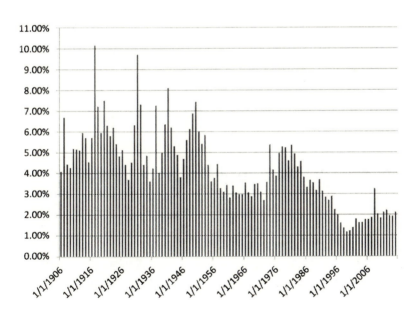

Figure 7.2: Average Dow Dividend Yield from 1906 to 2015

As the stock market has risen rapidly since 2009, higher-paying dividend stocks have once again become scarce. I believe that the dividend contribution to total return over the next decade will be closer to 2 percent, as I don't expect payout ratios to rise dramatically. This is a direct result of companies giving preference to stock buybacks and reinvesting their profits in capital expenditures.

Companies in today's era may be concerned about raising payout ratios back to historical levels due to the lack of growth since the go-go days of the 1990s. Despite companies' commitment to reinvesting their profits, earnings growth has not returned to the glory days of the 1990s (14 percent). Recent earnings growth has averaged 5 to 6 percent. Another factor is the price of stocks. Recall the Shiller CAPE P/E ratio mentioned in Chapter 1. As of June 2016, it is 26—among the top 10 percent readings in history and nearly 60 percent higher than the historical mean of 16.5. With a CAPE this high, future investment returns from stock-price appreciation are likely to be anemic.

Even if the stock market remains rosy, earning 2 percent from dividends versus 4 percent will most likely drive future investment returns below the 9 percent long-term average. I am of the opinion that dividends will most likely account for an outsized percentage of investment returns over the next decade.

Is the 2000 Secular Bear Really Over?

The Dow climbed above 18,000 in April 2016—far above the high marks for the Dow in 2000 (11,722) or even 2007 (14,164). So it may seem that the 2000 secular bear market has completed its journey.

However, history has demonstrated that if the Dow rises above the prior peak, but then drops back below it, a secular bear is not over. Recall that Chapter 1, I demonstrated that the Dow reached 103 in 1906 and then hit 119 in November 1919. But the Dow ultimately fell much further, bottoming out at 78 in January 1922. Thus, anyone who declared the secular bear market over in 1919 was ultimately proved wrong. Not until 1924 did the Dow rise above the 106 price level and never look back. Thus, 1924 was the official end of that elongated period of stock market stagnation.

Despite the fact that the average company now pays an average dividend yield far below the market average from 1906 to 1991, some companies still pay handsome dividends that allow snowball investors to earn decent total returns. I have scoured the US and international markets for just these kinds of companies.

I began with a long list (more than 2,500 companies) and gradually narrowed it down to my favorite 100 large-cap dividend companies. You'll find them all in Table 7.1, my Top 100 Snowball Investments. You can read full profiles of each company in the Appendix. Each company is ranked in its industry (category) based on five critical factors: dividend yield, dividend growth, P/E ratio, financial rating, and beta. I consider these five criteria to be the best way to evaluate dividend-paying firms. Firms with the highest ranking in each category earn the top position and the lowest score.

1-25	26-50	51-75	76-100
International Business Machines	Chubb Corp.	Siemens AG ADR	CVS CareMark
Wal-Mart Stores	Accenture PLC	Prudential Financial	Valero Energy
McDonald's Corp.	General Mills	TJX Companies	Sempra Energy
Nestle SA ADR	Southern Co	Union Pacific	Cardinal Health
Lockheed Martin	Toronto-Dominion Bank	Pepsico Inc.	Viacom 'B'
Chevron Corp.	AB Inbev ADR	Archer Daniels	Sysco Corp
Verizon	Marathon Petroleum Corp.	Eaton Corp.	Suncor Energy

Cisco Systems Inc.	Oracle Corp.	Nextera Energy	Ameriprise Financial
Occidental Petroleum	Royal Dutch Shell ADR	Texas Instruments	Boeing Company
Travelers Cos.	Discover Financial	Magna International	Pfizer, Inc.
AT&T Inc.	Emerson Electric	Aetna Inc.	Price (T. Rowe) Group
Teva Pharmaceuticals ADR	ConocoPhillips	Capital One Financial	Corning
Qualcomm	American Electric Power	Anthem Inc.	Dominion Res
Deere & Co.	UnitedHealth Group	Caterpillar Inc.	Automatic Data Proc.
Exxon Mobil Corp.	GlaxoSmithKline ADR	Infosys Technology ADR	Honeywell
Intel Corp.	Rio Tinto PLC ADR	Medtronic Inc.	MetLife Inc.
Amgen	Bank of Montreal	Ford Motor	Ventas Inc.
Procter & Gamble	Public Storage	Becton, Dickinson	Wells Fargo
Duke Energy	Kimberly-Clark	Stryker Corp.	3M
Raytheon	PPL Corp.	American Express	UPS
Bank of Nova Scotia	Target Corp.	Colgate-Palmolive	Diageo PLC ADR
Johnson & Johnson	Unilever Plc ADR	United Technology	J.P. Morgan Bank
Coca-Cola	Merck & Co.	Norfolk Southern	Maxim Integrated Products
Total ADR	Novartis AG ADR	Blackrock Inc.	KeyCorp
Microsoft Corp.	Kellogg Co.	Comcast	Apple Inc.

Table 7.1: Top 100 Snowball Investments (Dividend-Yielding Stocks)

For example, as you can see in Table 7.2, IBM ranks number one in its category (technology) based on its high average dividend yield, its above-average dividend growth, its low P/E ratio, its high S&P financial rating, and its low beta, and it has the lowest score in its category. In fact, IBM actually ranks among the top five companies for each measure, and its total score is the lowest of any stock that maintains a market cap of over $10 billion.

IBM (Technology)	Value	Score Ranking
Dividend Yield	3.00	78
Dividend Growth (5 year)	15	70
Trailing P/E	10.4	14
S&P Financial Rating	A++	40
Beta	0.90	100
Total Ranking in Technology	#1	302

Table 7.2: IBM Ranking Table (Top 100 Snowball Investments)

When putting together this list, I placed a great deal of focus on diversification. Astute investors must be sure to spread their funds among different sectors of the economy and different parts of the world. Many of the firms on the list are international companies, but you can find them on US exchanges as American depository receipts (ADRs).

Let's consider another example of the compounding value of the Top 100 Snowball Investment dividend-paying firms. Consider an investor with $100,001.20 to invest at the end of 2015. Like the investor who chose Pepsi in Chapter 3, this investor is focused on income and reinvestment to build his wealth. In this example, we'll assume that we continue on a secular bear market path that started in year 2000. In this example, the stock market does not advance over the coming decade (a potential outcome, given the current CAPE P/E ratio).

Table 7.3 shows the projected yearly dividends and growth the sample investor portfolio would deliver based on a starting value of $100,001.20 invested in the Top 100 Snowball Investment stocks. Each of the Top 100 pays a dividend each year. For simplicity's sake, I have chosen to reinvest those dividend proceeds into a single high-dividend ETF fund instead of each stock. Each firm's annual dividend and future dividends is based on the historical five-year growth rate in dividends for each company

ETFs (Exchange Traded Funds)

Introduced in 1993, ETFs are now one of the fastest-growing segments of the investment industry. ETFs are considered hybrid investment products; combining the diversification of mutual funds with the trading elements of common stocks. An investor in an ETF is looking for an interest in a pooled asset that maintains low overall expenses. Another advantage is that ETFs trade continuously throughout the day. An ETF can hold assets such as stocks, bonds, gold, currencies, etc. Most ETFs track an index, such as a stock or bond index. ETFs are attractive as investments because they let a small investor diversify quickly into dividend stocks at a low cost with excellent tax efficiency. Transparency is another key benefit because most ETF providers display their entire portfolios on a daily basis through their websites, If you are limited on the size of your portfolio, ETFs like the iShares Select Dividend ETF (Symbol: DVY) is a compelling choice. Other high dividend ETFs you may consider include the Schwab U.S. Dividend Equity ETF (SCHD), Vanguard Dividend Appreciation ETF (VIG), or the WisdomTree High Dividend Fund (DHS).

Here is the starting portfolio;

Total Shares Bought	Symbol	Company Name	Price	Value
10	AAPL	APPLE INC	$ 105.26	$ 1,053
10	ACN	ACCENTURE PLC	$ 104.50	$ 1,045
28	ADM	ARCHER DANIELS MIDLAND CO	$ 36.35	$ 1,018
12	ADP	AUTOMATIC DATA PROCESSING	$ 84.72	$ 1,017
17	AEP	AMERICAN ELECTRIC POWER INC	$ 57.75	$ 982

9	AET	AETNA INC NEW	$ 107.86	$ 971
6	AMGN	AMGEN INC	$ 161.21	$ 967
9	AMP	AMERIPRISE FINANCIAL INC	$ 105.52	$ 950
7	ANTM	ANTHEM INC COM	$ 139.44	$ 976
14	AXP	AMERICAN EXPRESS CO	$ 69.25	$ 970
7	BA	BOEING CO	$ 143.26	$ 1,003
6	BDX	BECTON DICKINSON CO	$ 154.09	$ 925
3	BLK	BLACKROCK, INC.	$ 340.52	$ 1,022
18	BMO	BANK OF MONTREAL	$ 56.42	$ 1,016
25	BNS	BANK OF NOVA SCOTIA	$ 40.44	$ 1,011
8	BUD	ANHEUSER BUSCH INBEV SA	$ 125.00	$ 1,000
11	CAH	CARDINAL HEALTH INC	$ 89.27	$ 982
15	CAT	CATERPILLAR INC	$ 67.12	$ 1,007
9	CB	CHUBB CORP	$ 116.85	$ 1,052
15	CL	COLGATE-PALMOLIVE CO	$ 66.62	$ 999
18	CMCSA	COMCAST CORP NEW CLA	$ 56.18	$ 1,011
14	COF	CAPITAL ONE FINANCIALCORP	$ 71.72	$ 1,004
21	COP	CONOCOPHILLIPS	$ 46.69	$ 980
37	CSCO	CISCO SYS INC COM	$ 27.15	$ 1,005
10	CVS	CVS CORPORATION	$ 97.33	$ 973
11	CVX	CHEVRON CORP NEW	$ 88.83	$ 977
15	D	DOMINION RESOURCES INC	$ 67.64	$ 1,015
13	DE	DEERE & COMPANY	$ 76.27	$ 992
9	DEO	DIAGEO ADR	$ 109.07	$ 982
19	DFS	DISCOVER FINL SVCS	$ 53.29	$ 1,013
14	DUK	DUKE ENERGY CORP	$ 71.39	$ 999
21	EMR	EMERSON ELECTRIC CO	$ 47.35	$ 994
19	ETN	EATON CORP PLC COM	$ 52.04	$ 989
71	F	FORD MTR CO DEL COM	$ 14.09	$ 1,000
17	GIS	GENERAL MILLS INCORPORATED	$ 57.21	$ 973
55	GLW	CORNING INC	$ 18.15	$ 998
25	GSK	GLAXOSMITHKLINE ADR	$ 40.35	$ 1,009

10	HON	HONEYWELL INTL INC	$ 102.98	$ 1,030
7	IBM	INTERNATIONAL BUSINESS MACHINES	$ 136.23	$ 954
60	INFY	INFOSYS TECHNOLOGIES LTD	$ 16.75	$ 1,005
29	INTC	INTEL CORP	$ 34.45	$ 999
10	JNJ	JOHNSON & JOHNSON	$ 102.72	$ 1,027
15	JPM	JPMORGAN CHASE & CO	$ 66.03	$ 990
14	K	KELLOGG COMPANY	$ 71.79	$ 1,005
76	KEY	KEYCORP NEW	$ 13.10	$ 996
8	KMB	KIMBERLY-CLARK CORP	$ 127.30	$ 1,018
23	KO	COCA COLA CO	$ 42.96	$ 988
5	LMT	LOCKHEED MARTIN CORP	$ 215.52	$ 1,078
9	MCD	MCDONALD'S CORPORATION	$ 117.25	$ 1,055
13	MDT	MEDTRONIC PLC	$ 76.92	$ 1,000
21	MET	METLIFE INC COM	$ 47.79	$ 1,004
25	MGA	MAGNA INTL INC CL A	$ 40.56	$ 1,014
7	MMM	3M COMPANY	$ 149.56	$ 1,047
19	MPC	MARATHON PETROLEUM CORP	$ 51.30	$ 975
19	MRK	MERCK & CO INC NEW COM	$ 52.82	$ 1,004
18	MSFT	MICROSOFT CORP	$ 55.48	$ 999
26	MXIM	MAXIM INTEGRATED PRODSINC	$ 38.00	$ 988
10	NEE	NEXTERA ENERFY INC.	$ 103.11	$ 1,031
11	NSC	NORFOLK SOUTHERN CRP	$ 83.84	$ 922
13	NSRGY	NESTLE S A SPONS ADR	$ 74.42	$ 967
12	NVS	NOVARTIS A G	$ 82.81	$ 994
27	ORCL	ORACLE CORP	$ 36.53	$ 986
15	OXY	OCCIDENTAL PETROLEUM CORP	$ 67.61	$ 1,014
10	PEP	PEPSICO INC	$ 99.92	$ 999
31	PFE	PFIZER INC	$ 32.28	$ 1,001
13	PG	PROCTER & GAMBLE CO	$ 79.41	$ 1,032
29	PPL	PPL CORP	$ 34.13	$ 990
12	PRU	PRUDENTIAL FINL INC	$ 80.55	$ 967

4	PSA	PUBLIC STORAGE	$ 247.70	$ 991
20	QCOM	QUALCOMM INC	$ 49.53	$ 991
22	RDSB	ROYAL DUTCH SHELL PLC	$ 46.04	$ 1,013
36	RIO	RIO TINTO ADS	$ 28.00	$ 1,008
8	RTN	RAYTHEON CO COM NEW	$ 123.86	$ 991
11	SIEGY	SIEMENS A G SPONSORED ADR	$ 92.16	$ 1,014
21	SO	SOUTHERN CO	$ 46.79	$ 983
11	SRE	SEMPRA ENERGY	$ 94.01	$ 1,034
39	SU	SUNCOR ENERGY	$ 25.80	$ 1,006
11	SYK	STRYKER CORP	$ 92.94	$ 1,022
25	SYY	SYSCO CORP	$ 40.69	$ 1,017
29	T	AT&T INC COM	$ 34.41	$ 998
26	TD	THE TORONTO-DOMINION BANK	$ 38.80	$ 1,009
15	TEVA	TEVA PHARMACEUTICAL	$ 65.64	$ 985
14	TGT	TARGET CORP	$ 72.61	$ 1,017
14	TJX	TJX COMPANIES INC	$ 70.69	$ 990
22	TOT	TOTAL S A	$ 44.95	$ 989
14	TROW	ROWE T PRICE GROUP INC	$ 71.49	$ 1,001
9	TRV	TRAVELERS COMPANIES INC	$ 112.86	$ 1,016
18	TXN	TEXAS INSTRUMENTS INC	$ 54.81	$ 987
23	UL	UNILEVER PLC SPONSORED ADR	$ 42.80	$ 984
9	UNH	UNITEDHEALTH GROUP	$ 117.64	$ 1,059
13	UNP	UNION PACIFIC CORP	$ 77.66	$ 1,010
10	UPS	UNITED PARCEL SVC INC	$ 96.23	$ 962
10	UTX	UNITED TECHNOLOGIES CORP	$ 95.36	$ 954
24	VIAB	VIACOM INC NEW CL B	$ 41.16	$ 988
14	VLO	VALERO ENERGY CORP	$ 70.02	$ 980
18	VTR	VENTAS INC	$ 56.43	$ 1,016
22	VZ	VERIZON COMMUNICATIONS	$ 46.22	$ 1,017
19	WFC	WELLS FARGO COMPANY COM	$ 53.94	$ 1,025
16	WMT	WALMART STORES INC	$ 61.30	$ 981

13	XOM	EXXON MOBIL CORP	$ 77.95	$ 1,013
Total Portfolio Value				**$100,001.20**

Table 7.3: Sample Initial Dividend Investor
Portfolio as of December 31, 2015

Table 7.4 shows the yearly dividends and growth delivered by this sample investor portfolio, based on each firm's historical five-year growth rate in dividends for the first five years.

Symbol	Dividends + Interest				
	2016	2017	2018	2019	2020
AAPL	$23.09	$25.63	$28.45	$31.58	$35.05
ACN	$23.76	$25.66	$27.71	$29.93	$32.33
ADM	$35.95	$38.47	$41.16	$44.04	$47.13
ADP	$27.48	$29.67	$32.05	$34.61	$37.38
AEP	$40.36	$42.79	$45.35	$48.08	$50.96
AET	$9.99	$11.09	$12.31	$13.66	$15.17
AMGN	$30.48	$38.71	$49.16	$62.43	$79.29
AMP	$27.98	$32.46	$37.65	$43.67	$50.66
ANTM	$21.29	$24.91	$29.15	$34.10	$39.90
AXP	$18.19	$20.37	$22.82	$25.55	$28.62
BA	$36.62	$43.95	$52.74	$63.29	$75.94
BDX	$17.42	$19.17	$21.08	$23.19	$25.51
BLK	$31.05	$35.09	$39.65	$44.81	$50.63
BMO	$62.90	$65.42	$68.03	$70.75	$73.58
BNS	$76.30	$83.17	$90.65	$98.81	$107.70
BUD	$34.27	$41.46	$50.17	$60.71	$73.45
CAH	$19.24	$21.74	$24.57	$27.76	$31.37
CAT	$50.82	$55.90	$61.49	$67.64	$74.41
CB	$21.14	$21.77	$22.42	$23.10	$23.79
CL	$24.17	$25.62	$27.16	$28.78	$30.51
CMCSA	$21.98	$24.40	$27.08	$30.06	$33.36
COF	$29.79	$39.62	$52.70	$70.09	$93.22
COP	$22.05	$23.15	$24.31	$25.53	$26.80

CSCO	$42.71	$47.41	$52.63	$58.42	$64.84
CVS	$20.57	$24.89	$30.12	$36.44	$44.09
CVX	$50.38	$53.90	$57.68	$61.71	$66.03
D	$45.36	$48.99	$52.91	$57.14	$61.71
DE	$36.82	$43.44	$51.26	$60.49	$71.38
DEO	$26.21	$29.35	$32.88	$36.82	$41.24
DFS	$24.90	$29.13	$34.08	$39.88	$46.66
DUK	$48.05	$49.97	$51.97	$54.05	$56.21
EMR	$43.49	$47.41	$51.67	$56.32	$61.39
ETN	$48.52	$54.34	$60.86	$68.16	$76.34
F	$51.55	$62.37	$75.47	$91.32	$110.49
GIS	$32.01	$34.26	$36.65	$39.22	$41.96
GLW	$33.56	$37.92	$42.85	$48.43	$54.72
GSK	$81.74	$99.72	$121.66	$148.43	$181.08
HON	$27.37	$31.48	$36.20	$41.63	$47.87
IBM	$42.95	$50.68	$59.81	$70.57	$83.27
INFY	$71.21	$91.86	$118.50	$152.86	$197.19
INTC	$32.57	$35.18	$37.99	$41.03	$44.31
JNJ	$32.10	$34.35	$36.75	$39.32	$42.08
JPM	$29.04	$31.94	$35.14	$38.65	$42.52
K	$28.56	$29.13	$29.71	$30.31	$30.91
KEY	$26.22	$30.15	$34.68	$39.88	$45.86
KMB	$30.91	$32.46	$34.08	$35.78	$37.57
KO	$34.78	$37.56	$40.56	$43.81	$47.31
LMT	$36.30	$39.93	$43.92	$48.32	$53.15
MCD	$33.64	$35.32	$37.09	$38.94	$40.89
MDT	$24.70	$30.88	$38.59	$48.24	$60.30
MET	$33.71	$36.06	$38.59	$41.29	$44.18
MGA	$29.00	$33.64	$39.02	$45.27	$52.51
MMM	$33.57	$36.25	$39.15	$42.28	$45.67
MPC	$31.13	$39.85	$51.00	$65.28	$83.56
MRK	$35.66	$36.37	$37.10	$37.84	$38.60
MSFT	$30.07	$34.88	$40.46	$46.93	$54.44
MXIM	$33.38	$35.72	$38.22	$40.90	$43.76
NEE	$39.32	$44.44	$50.21	$56.74	$64.12
NSC	$27.00	$28.08	$29.20	$30.37	$31.58

NSRGY	$32.61	$36.20	$40.18	$44.60	$49.51
NVS	$34.44	$35.82	$37.26	$38.75	$40.30
ORCL	$20.25	$25.31	$31.64	$39.55	$49.44
OXY	$46.80	$48.67	$50.62	$52.64	$54.75
PEP	$30.07	$32.17	$34.42	$36.83	$39.41
PFE	$39.80	$42.59	$45.57	$48.76	$52.17
PG	$35.48	$36.55	$37.64	$38.77	$39.94
PPL	$44.96	$45.86	$46.78	$47.71	$48.67
PRU	$40.66	$49.19	$59.52	$72.02	$87.15
PSA	$32.91	$39.82	$48.19	$58.31	$70.55
QCOM	$43.78	$49.90	$56.89	$64.86	$73.94
RDSB	$78.71	$81.86	$85.13	$88.53	$92.08
RIO	$85.14	$93.65	$103.02	$113.32	$124.65
RTN	$23.80	$26.42	$29.32	$32.55	$36.13
SIEGY	$41.66	$42.08	$42.50	$42.92	$43.35
SO	$46.94	$48.35	$49.80	$51.29	$52.83
SRE	$35.21	$37.33	$39.57	$41.94	$44.46
SU	$55.19	$67.34	$82.15	$100.22	$122.27
SYK	$18.39	$20.23	$22.25	$24.48	$26.93
SYY	$31.93	$32.89	$33.87	$34.89	$35.94
T	$56.79	$57.93	$59.09	$60.27	$61.48
TD	$59.49	$61.87	$64.34	$66.92	$69.59
TEVA	$21.62	$22.92	$24.30	$25.75	$27.30
TGT	$33.87	$36.58	$39.50	$42.66	$46.08
TJX	$14.11	$16.93	$20.32	$24.39	$29.26
TOT	$59.69	$60.88	$62.10	$63.34	$64.61
TROW	$35.68	$42.11	$49.69	$58.63	$69.18
TRV	$24.38	$27.06	$30.03	$33.34	$37.00
TXN	$30.64	$34.32	$38.44	$43.05	$48.22
UL	$31.88	$33.47	$35.15	$36.90	$38.75
UNH	$23.94	$31.84	$42.35	$56.32	$74.91
UNP	$31.46	$34.61	$38.07	$41.87	$46.06
UPS	$33.38	$35.72	$38.22	$40.90	$43.76
UTX	$27.65	$29.86	$32.25	$34.83	$37.61
VIAB	$46.46	$56.22	$68.03	$82.31	$99.60
VLO	$40.32	$48.38	$58.06	$69.67	$83.61

VTR	$71.48	$97.21	$132.21	$179.81	$244.54
VZ	$51.21	$52.75	$54.33	$55.96	$57.64
WFC	$30.50	$32.63	$34.91	$37.36	$39.97
WMT	$32.64	$33.29	$33.96	$34.64	$35.33
	XOM $40.24 $42.65 $45.21			$47.92	$50.80
DVY*	$0.00	$127.80	$274.76	$444.10	$639.72
	Shares				
DVY Share Purchases on 12/31	0	73	84	97	112
Total Income	$3,651.55	$4,198.79	$4,838.17	$5,589.15	$6,476.06

Table 7.4: Sample Portfolio Dividend Projections, 2016–2020
* All proceeds from dividends are used to buy additional shares of the iShares Select Dividend ETF (Symbol: DVY) at the end of each year. DVY shares collected will also pay out an annual dividend, as seen in this and the following table. The projections for DVY dividends per year are based upon the historical increases for the previous five years.

Table 7.5 continues this analysis, showing the yearly dividends and growth delivered by this sample investor portfolio from 2021 to 2025.

Symbol	Dividends + Interest				
	2021	2022	2023	2024	2025
AAPL	$38.90	$43.18	$47.93	$53.21	$59.06
ACN	$34.91	$37.70	$40.72	$43.98	$47.50
ADM	$50.42	$53.95	$57.73	$61.77	$66.10
ADP	$40.37	$43.60	$47.09	$50.85	$54.92
AEP	$54.02	$57.26	$60.69	$64.34	$68.20
AET	$16.83	$18.69	$20.74	$23.02	$25.55
AMGN	$100.70	$127.89	$162.42	$206.27	$261.97
AMP	$58.77	$68.17	$79.08	$91.73	$106.40

ANTM	$46.69	$54.62	$63.91	$74.77	$87.48
AXP	$32.05	$35.90	$40.21	$45.03	$50.44
BA	$91.13	$109.36	$131.23	$157.48	$188.97
BDX	$28.06	$30.87	$33.95	$37.35	$41.08
BLK	$57.21	$64.65	$73.05	$82.55	$93.28
BMO	$76.53	$79.59	$82.77	$86.08	$89.53
BNS	$117.40	$127.96	$139.48	$152.03	$165.72
BUD	$88.88	$107.55	$130.13	$157.46	$190.52
CAH	$35.45	$40.06	$45.27	$51.15	$57.80
CAT	$81.85	$90.03	$99.03	$108.94	$119.83
CB	$24.50	$25.24	$25.99	$26.77	$27.58
CL	$32.34	$34.28	$36.34	$38.52	$40.83
CMCSA	$37.03	$41.11	$45.63	$50.65	$56.22
COF	$123.98	$164.90	$219.31	$291.68	$387.94
COP	$28.14	$29.55	$31.03	$32.58	$34.21
CSCO	$71.97	$79.89	$88.68	$98.43	$109.26
CVS	$53.35	$64.56	$78.11	$94.52	$114.37
CVX	$70.65	$75.60	$80.89	$86.55	$92.61
D	$66.65	$71.98	$77.74	$83.96	$90.67
DE	$84.23	$99.39	$117.28	$138.39	$163.30
DEO	$46.19	$51.73	$57.94	$64.89	$72.68
DFS	$54.59	$63.87	$74.72	$87.43	$102.29
DUK	$58.46	$60.80	$63.23	$65.76	$68.39
EMR	$66.92	$72.94	$79.50	$86.66	$94.46
ETN	$85.51	$95.77	$107.26	$120.13	$134.55
F	$133.70	$161.77	$195.75	$236.85	$286.59
GIS	$44.90	$48.04	$51.41	$55.01	$58.86
GLW	$61.83	$69.87	$78.96	$89.22	$100.82
GSK	$220.92	$269.52	$328.82	$401.16	$489.41
HON	$55.05	$63.31	$72.80	$83.73	$96.28
IBM	$98.26	$115.95	$136.82	$161.45	$190.51
INFY	$254.38	$328.15	$423.31	$546.07	$704.43
INTC	$47.86	$51.69	$55.82	$60.29	$65.11
JNJ	$45.02	$48.17	$51.55	$55.15	$59.01
JPM	$46.77	$51.45	$56.59	$62.25	$68.47
K	$31.53	$32.16	$32.81	$33.46	$34.13

KEY	$52.74	$60.65	$69.75	$80.21	$92.24
KMB	$39.45	$41.43	$43.50	$45.67	$47.95
KO	$51.10	$55.19	$59.60	$64.37	$69.52
LMT	$58.46	$64.31	$70.74	$77.81	$85.59
MCD	$42.94	$45.08	$47.34	$49.70	$52.19
MDT	$75.38	$94.22	$117.78	$147.22	$184.03
MET	$47.27	$50.58	$54.12	$57.91	$61.97
MGA	$60.91	$70.66	$81.96	$95.07	$110.29
MMM	$49.32	$53.27	$57.53	$62.13	$67.10
MPC	$106.96	$136.91	$175.24	$224.31	$287.12
MRK	$39.37	$40.16	$40.96	$41.78	$42.62
MSFT	$63.15	$73.26	$84.98	$98.57	$114.34
MXIM	$46.82	$50.10	$53.61	$57.36	$61.38
NEE	$72.45	$81.87	$92.51	$104.54	$118.13
NSC	$32.85	$34.16	$35.53	$36.95	$38.43
NSRGY	$54.95	$61.00	$67.71	$75.16	$83.42
NVS	$41.91	$43.58	$45.33	$47.14	$49.03
ORCL	$61.80	$77.25	$96.56	$120.70	$150.87
OXY	$56.94	$59.22	$61.59	$64.05	$66.61
PEP	$42.17	$45.12	$48.28	$51.66	$55.28
PFE	$55.83	$59.74	$63.92	$68.39	$73.18
PG	$41.14	$42.37	$43.64	$44.95	$46.30
PPL	$49.64	$50.63	$51.65	$52.68	$53.73
PRU	$105.45	$127.60	$154.39	$186.81	$226.04
PSA	$85.37	$103.29	$124.98	$151.23	$182.99
QCOM	$84.29	$96.09	$109.54	$124.87	$142.36
RDSB	$95.76	$99.59	$103.57	$107.72	$112.02
RIO	$137.12	$150.83	$165.91	$182.51	$200.76
RTN	$40.10	$44.51	$49.41	$54.84	$60.88
SIEGY	$43.79	$44.23	$44.67	$45.11	$45.57
SO	$54.41	$56.05	$57.73	$59.46	$61.24
SRE	$47.12	$49.95	$52.95	$56.12	$59.49
SU	$149.17	$181.99	$222.02	$270.87	$330.46
SYK	$29.62	$32.58	$35.84	$39.42	$43.37
SYY	$37.02	$38.13	$39.27	$40.45	$41.66
T	$62.70	$63.96	$65.24	$66.54	$67.87

TD	$72.38	$75.27	$78.28	$81.41	$84.67
TEVA	$28.94	$30.67	$32.51	$34.47	$36.53
TGT	$49.76	$53.75	$58.05	$62.69	$67.70
TJX	$35.12	$42.14	$50.57	$60.68	$72.81
TOT	$65.90	$67.22	$68.57	$69.94	$71.34
TROW	$81.63	$96.33	$113.67	$134.13	$158.27
TRV	$41.07	$45.59	$50.61	$56.17	$62.35
TXN	$54.00	$60.48	$67.74	$75.87	$84.98
UL	$40.69	$42.72	$44.86	$47.10	$49.45
UNH	$99.63	$132.51	$176.23	$234.39	$311.74
UNP	$50.67	$55.73	$61.31	$67.44	$74.18
UPS	$46.82	$50.10	$53.61	$57.36	$61.38
UTX	$40.62	$43.87	$47.38	$51.17	$55.27
VIAB	$120.52	$145.82	$176.45	$213.50	$258.34
VLO	$100.33	$120.39	$144.47	$173.37	$208.04
VTR	$332.57	$452.30	$615.13	$836.58	$1,037.74
VZ	$59.37	$61.15	$62.98	$64.87	$66.82
WFC	$42.77	$45.76	$48.97	$52.40	$56.06
WMT	$36.04	$36.76	$37.49	$38.24	$39.01
XOM	$53.85	$57.08	$60.50	$64.13	$67.98
DVY	$866.38	$1,129.91	$1,437.48	$1,797.98	$2,222.45
Total DVY Shares Owned	496	647	823	1030	1273
	Shares				
DVY Share Purchases on 12/31 of each year	121	138	158	183	214
Total Income	$7,529.44	$8,787.80	$10,299.91	$12,127.77	$14,350.48

Table 7.5: Sample Portfolio Dividend Projections, 2021–2025

Although the prices of all the stocks and the DVY ETF held in the portfolio stagnated from 2016 through 2025, the portfolio's value continued to grow the original investment, $100,001.20, to \$163,498.85 by the end of 2025—a 4.99 percent annual total return.

By reinvesting the dividends each year back into the DVY exchange-traded fund (ETF), the investor's number of shares in the ETF grew from zero to 1,273. As a result, the total yearly income of this portfolio skyrocketed over the decade from an initial \$3,651 per year to \$14,350 per year.

The initial yield on the investor's portfolio was 3.65 percent, based on his investment of \$100,001.20 and the annual dividends that would be collected as income. But just ten years later, the investment produced over three times that amount—yielding 14.3 percent (\$14,350.48/\$100,001.20) based on the original investment's value. An investor following this path of dividend collection and reinvestment can be assured that they will be rewarded even during future periods of stock market stagnation.

CREATING YOUR OWN SNOWBALL EFFECT

Today, we live in a world of 24-hour business television, high-speed trading, and volatile capital markets. Instead of asking your dentist for a hot stock tip, you need only turn on the TV to hear what the talking heads recommend or jump on the Internet to find thousands of web pages devoted to showing you how to make a quick buck. Don't listen to pundits and faceless Internet "experts." Consider instead the proof I've provided in this book.

There is no easy way to build wealth without taking on substantial risk—especially if you are highly dependent on stocks to increase in price as your only method of profit. If you want true wealth building, and most of us do, follow the methodology I've put forth here. Remember: *Companies that pay dividends will always provide you with a return. Always.* You don't need to examine your stocks' price movement each day or panic when you hear on the news that the Dow fell by 500 points. Instead, concentrate your attention on the power of compounding dividends over time and their ability to provide income on and add value to *the shares you collect and already own,* not the price of your shares at any given moment in time. Remember the story of the sale of Manhattan? A Native American tribe sold the island to the West India Company for a mere pittance—60 guilders (the equivalent of $24 in US dollars)—back in 1626. If you had taken that measly sum and invested it in a dividend-paying stock at a 5 percent yield and a growth rate in dividends per year of 5 percent, your sum in 2015 would be worth more than $10,000 trillion. Now that's a snowball!

The historic examples I've provided in *The Snowball Effect* are meant to convey the power of putting your money in investments that produce income. You can never guess which way the Dow will go over the next thirty years, but you *can* count on those quarterly payments to build up your nest egg. Tables 7.4 and 7.5 clearly demonstrate the power of the reinvestment of stock dividends during a period of stock-market stagnation.

Now, it's time for you to put this strategy to use. It doesn't matter whether you start with $100 or $100,000—the key is to get started as soon as possible with the process of building wealth through reinvestment of dividends and interest.

Dividend-bearing stocks. You can choose to start with my Top 100 Snowball Investment stocks listed in Table 7.1 and explored in depth in the appendix, or review websites like Yahoo! Finance to collect information on other dividend-paying companies that interest you.

Even if you start with a small amount of funds, consider directly investing in dividend-paying companies yourself or using a large discount brokerage, such as Charles Schwab or Scottrade. In my opinion, the most important thing is to start your investing with as many of the Top 100 Snowball Investment firms as possible. As each firm pays its dividend, reinvest those cash payments into the same firm if its selling at a discount, or select another company within the Top 100 that offers a high relative dividend yield (as shown in Chapter 3's Pepsi example). You may also consider micro-cap dividend stocks as well for diversification. I have provided a list of micro-cap dividend stocks that may warrant attention in the Appendix.

Bonds. Bonds provide diversification from your stock holdings and consistent semi-annual coupon payments. If you are interested in investing in bonds but have a relatively small portfolio, choose an ETF instead of investing in individual corporate bonds. Newly issued individual corporate bonds are priced at $1,000 per bond (or close to it), so an ETF will allow you to spread risk among many issuers. As your portfolio grows, or if you are starting with a larger pool of funds, you can buy individual corporate bonds. You can learn much about individual bonds at www.bondsonline. com or through large discount brokerages, which generally have an inventory of bonds available for purchase. Remember: Concentrate your holdings on bonds rated BBB and BB to get the best yields with minimal risk. You may choose from the list of 50 solid companies provided in Chapter 5 or the ETFs that are presented in the Appendix.

Lastly, utilize covered calls when prudent, to generate additional income along the way. This will increase your "snowball' by allowing you to buy additional shares of stock or bonds. For another example, in the appendix each Top 100 company is listed along with a ten year history of average dividend yield. Here is the IBM table;

Date	Yearly Dividend	Dividend Growth %	Average Dividend Yield %
2015	5.00	15	3.2
2014	4.25	23	2.7
2013	3.70	12	2.0
2012	3.30	14	1.7
2011	2.90	16	1.6
2010	2.50	16	1.7
2009	2.15	13	1.6
2008	1.90	27	2.3
2007	1.50	36	1.4
2006	1.10	41	1.1
2005	0.78	11	1.0

Table 7.6: Dividend Table from Top 100 Source: IBM

With your covered call income, you will normally not buy more shares of the same firm you wrote covered calls against. The reason is that the price of the stock was high and the dividend yield below average. That is why any prudent investor would write a covered call in the first place. I would recommend you examine the Top 100 for firms that trade at a lower valuation and higher dividend yield. For example, you could attempt to buy additional shares of IBM based upon the fact that its yield remains above 3 percent in 2016, which is much above its long-term average. Thus, it presents a compelling reinvestment opportunity.

Good luck to you! Now that you know the building blocks to consistent income and reinvestment, your investment future can be much more of a certainty.

BIBLIOGRAPHY

Asness, Cliff, Andrea Frazzini, Ronen Israel, Tobias Maskowitz, and Lasse Pedersen. "Size Matters If You Control the Junk." Working Paper, 2015, 32–34.

Banz, R. "The Relationship between Return and Market Value of Common Stocks." *Journal of Financial Economics* (1981): 9(1): 3–18.

Black, F. "The Dividend Puzzle." *Journal of Portfolio Management* 2 (1976): 5–8.

Cassidy, Donald. *When the Dow Breaks*. McGraw-Hill, 1999.

Campbell, John Y. "Asset Pricing at the Millennium." *Journal of Finance* 55 (2000): 1515–1567.

Credit Suisse. *Credit Suisse Global Investment Returns Yearbook*, 2016.

DeAngelo, H., L. DeAngelo, and D. Skinner. "Are Dividends Disappearing? Dividend Concentration and the Consolidation of Earnings." *Journal of Financial Economics* 72 (2004): 425–456.

Easterday, Kathryn E., Pradyot K. Sen, and Jens A. Stephan. "The Persistence of the Small Firm/January Effect: Is It Consistent with Investors' Learning and Arbitrage Efforts?" *The Quarterly Review of Economics and Finance*, 49 (2009): 1172–1193.

Fama, E. and K. French. "Disappearing Dividends: Changing Firm Characteristics or Lower Propensity to Pay?" *Journal of Financial Economics* 60 (2001a): 3–43.

Frankfurter, G.M. "What Is the Puzzle in 'The Dividend Puzzle?'" *The Journal of Investing* 8 (1999): 76–85.

Geske, Robert L. and Gordon Delianedis. "The Components of Corporate Credit Spreads: Default, Recovery, Taxes, Jumps, Liquidity, and Market Factors." UCLA Anderson Working Paper, 2001. No. 22-01.

Gompers, P.A., and A. Metrick. "Institutional Investors and Equity Prices." *Quarterly Journal of Economics* 116 (2001): 229–259.

Gordon, M.J. "Dividends, Earnings, and Stock Prices." *Review of Economics and Statistics* 41 (1959): 99–105.

Hawakini, Gabriel and Donald B. Keim. "The Cross Section of Common Stock Returns: A Review of the Evidence and Some New Findings." Rodney L. White Center for Financial Research, Wharton School: 1999.

Hempel, George H. *The Postwar Quality of State and Local Debt.* NBER, 1971.

Houweling, Patrick, Albert Mentink, and Ton Vorst. "Comparing Possible Proxies of Corporate Bond Liquidity." *Journal of Banking and Finance* 29 (2005): 1331–1358.

Huang, Jing-zhi and Ming Huang. "How Much of the Corporate–Treasury Yield Spread Is Due to Credit Risk?" Stanford University Working Paper, 2002. No. FIN-02-04.

Kealhofer, Stephen, Sherry Kwok, and Wenlong Weng. "Uses and Abuses of Bond Default Rates." Document Number: 999-0000-039.

Keim, Donald. "Size-Related Anomalies and Stock Return Seasonality," *Journal of Financial Economics,* (1983), 12: 13–32.

Kozhemiakin, A. "The Risk Premium of Corporate Bonds." *The Journal of Portfolio Management* 33(2) (2007): 101–109.

Lewellen, Jonathan. "Institutional Investors and the Limits of Arbitrage." *Journal of Financial Economics* 102(1) (2011): 63–64.

Liu, Weimin. "A Liquidity-Augmented Capital Asset Pricing Model." *Journal of Financial Economics* 82(3) (2006): 631–671.

Money Market Reform Presentation, Stradley & Ranon, Crane Data 2015.

Morningstar. *Ibbotson SBBI 2015 Classic Yearbook: Market Results for Stocks, Bonds, Bills, and Inflation.* Morningstar: Chicago, 2015.

Options Clearing Corporation. "TradeKing Options Playbook." https://investor.tradeking.com/PrivateView/edu/opb/opbCashingOutYourOptions.tmpl (accessed May 9, 2016).

al Rjoub, S. and M.K. Hassan. "Transaction Cost and the Small Stock Puzzle: The Impact of Outliers in the NYSE, 1970–2000." *International Journal of Applied Econometrics and Quantitative Studies* 1(3) (2004), 103–114.

Royce Funds, The. "The Importance of Small-Cap Investing." https://www.roycefunds.com/insights/whitepapers/dividends-crucial-component-long-term-investment-approach (accessed April 27, 2016).

Sawicki, Julia, Nilanjan Sen, and Cheah Chee Yian. "The Disappearance of the Small Stock Premium: Size as a Narrowly-Held Risk." 2005. 2–3.

Shell, Ada. "Financial Crisis Ushers in 'The Age of Safety' for Investors." *USA Today*, September 4, 2012. Accessed at: http://usatoday30.usatoday.com/money/markets/story/2012-09-04/investing-stocks-safety-risk/57582840/1, May 28, 2016.

Siegel, Jeremy J. *Stocks for the Long Run.* New York: McGraw-Hill, 2002. 78–80.

Wasik, John F. "Retirement Investors, Riding Out the Panic." *New York Times*, October 9, 2015. Accessed at: http://www.nytimes.com/2015/10/11/business/mutfund/retirement-investors-riding-out-the-panic.html?_r=0, May 28, 2016.

INDEX

Page numbers in italics refer to figures and tables.

SUGGESTIONS FOR ADDITIONAL READING

Get Rich with Dividends: A Proven System for Earning Double-Digit Returns
Feb 24, 2015
by Marc Lichtenfeld

The Little Book of Big Dividends: A Safe Formula for Guaranteed Returns
Feb 8, 2010
by Charles B. Carlson and Terry Savage

The Strategic Dividend Investor
Apr 18, 2011
by Daniel Peris

Beating the S&P with Dividends: How to Build a Superior Portfolio of Dividend Yielding Stocks
Mar 14, 2005
by Peter O'Shea and Jonathan Worrall

A Random Walk Down Wall Street: The Time-Tested Strategy for Successful Investing (11th Edition)
Jan 4, 2016
by Burton G. Malkiel

What Works on Wall Street, Fourth Edition: The Classic Guide to the Best-Performing Investment Strategies
Nov 14, 2011
by James O'Shaughnessy

The Ivy Portfolio: How to Invest Like the Top Endowments and Avoid Bear Markets
Apr 5, 2011
by Mebane T. Faber and Eric W. Richardson

Security Analysis: The Classic 1934 Edition
Oct 22, 1996
by Benjamin Graham and David Dodd

Stocks for the Long Run 5th Edition: The Definitive Guide to Financial Market Returns & Long-Term Investment Strategies
Jan 7, 2014
by Jeremy J. Siegel

One Up On Wall Street: How To Use What You Already Know To Make Money In The Market
Apr 9, 2001
by Peter Lynch and John Rothchild

The Little Book of Common Sense Investing: The Only Way to Guarantee Your Fair Share of Stock Market Returns
Mar 5, 2007
by John C. Bogle

Bonds Now!: Making Money in the New Fixed Income Landscape
Dec 9, 2009
by Marilyn Cohen and Christopher R. Malburg

The Only Guide to a Winning Bond Strategy You'll Ever Need: The Way Smart Money Preserves Wealth Today Hardcover
March 7, 2006
by Larry E. Swedroe

Asset Allocation: Balancing Financial Risk, Fifth Edition Hardcover
May 21, 2013
by Roger Gibson (Author)

ETF CORPORATE BOND RECOMMENDATIONS

Symbol	Name	Type
QLTB	iShares Baa - Ba Rated Corporate Bond	ETF
CORP	PIMCO Investment Grade Corporate Bond Index ETF	ETF
VCSH	Vanguard Short-Term Corporate Bond ETF	ETF
VCLT	Vanguard Long-Term Corporate Bond ETF	ETF
CRDT	WisdomTree Strategic Corporate Bond ETF	ETF
GHYG	iShares Global High Yield Corporate Bond	ETF
FCOR	Fidelity Corporate Bond ETF	ETF
QLTB	iShares Baa - Ba Rated Corporate Bond	ETF
GLCB	WisdomTree Strategic Corporate Bond ETF	ETF
HYG	iShares iBoxx $ High Yield Corporate Bond ETF	ETF

MICRO-CAP DIVIDEND STOCK RECOMMENDATIONS

Company	Market Cap	Dividend Yield	Symbol
Allegheny Valley Bancorp Inc.	42.37M	4.45	AVLY
Ardmore Shipping Corporation	258.54M	8.83	ASC
Ballston Spa Bancorp, Inc.	25.04M	3.68	BSPA
BEO Bancorp	20.71M	2.98	BEOB
Blue Capital Reinsurance Holdings Ltd.	150.98M	7.01	BCRH
Capella Education Co.	598.91M	3.01	CPLA
Cass Information Systems, Inc.	567.18M	1.76	CASS
CBT Financial Corp.	27.16M	4.4	CBTC
Chicago Rivet & Machine Co.	27.24M	2.63	CVR
Citi Trends, Inc.	239.56M	1.47	CTRN
Citizens Bancorp of Virginia Inc.	47.63M	3.88	CZBT
Clifton Bancorp Inc.	340.56M	1.6	CSBK
CNB Corp.	20.79M	2.92	CNBZ
Commercial Bancshares, Inc.	39.11M	3.19	CMOH
Computer Task Group Inc.	81.77M	4.74	CTG
Consumers Bancorp Inc.	47.05M	2.79	CBKM
Corning Natural Gas Holding Corporation	42.02M	3.63	CNIG
CryoLife Inc.	386.47M	1.02	CRY
Culp, Inc.	347.67M	1.12	CFI
Detrex Corp.	45.25M	3.7	DTRX

Eagle Bancorp Montana, Inc.	46.87M	2.42	EBMT
Ecology & Environment, Inc.	43.035M	4.91	EEI
Elmira Savings Bank	51.58M	4.58	ESBK
Empire Resources Inc.	31M	2.82	ERS
FBR & Co.	119.83M	4.99	FBRC
First Century Bankshares Inc.	39.01M	3.9	FCBS
First Colebrook Bancorp, Inc.	13.32M	2.74	FCNH
First Federal of N. Michigan Bancorp	26.09M	2.29	FFNM
First Robinson Financial Corp.	16.19M	2.95	FRFC
First West Virginia Bancorp Inc.	31.55M	4.53	FWVB
FreightCar America Inc.	175.64M	2.46	RAIL
FutureFuel Corp.	453.39M	2.3	FF
GAIN Capital Holdings, Inc.	310.09M	3.15	GCAP
George Risk Industries Inc.	37.43M	4.56	RSKIA
Glen Burnie Bancorp	29.99M	3.7	GLBZ
Global Self Storage, Inc.	40.64M	5.07	SELF
GNB Financial Services, Inc.	31.56M	1.6	GNBF
Graham Corporation	180.01M	1.97	GHM
Haynes International, Inc.	367.33M	2.81	HAYN
Heidrick & Struggles International Inc.	327.79M	2.99	HSII
Highlands Bankshares Inc.	37.55M	3.64	HBSI
Home City Financial Corp.	15.34M	2.24	HCFL
Home Financial Bancorp	8.63M	2.21	HWEN
International Shipholding Corp.	2.14M	69.2	ISHC
Jacksonville Bancorp Inc.	46.59M	1.48	JXSB
JMP Group LLC	116.65M	6.47	JMP
Kadant Inc.	549.79M	1.53	KAI
Katahdin Bankshares Corp.	38.26M	3.53	KTHN
Kewaunee Scientific Corp.	50.31M	3.11	KEQU
Kforce Inc.	463.71M	2.74	KFRC
Landauer Inc.	386.82M	2.76	LDR
Landmark Bancorp, Inc.	19.84M	2.64	LDKB
Ledyard Financial Group, Inc.	48.99M	4.02	LFGP
Limoneira Company	251.66M	1.1	LMNR

LSI Industries Inc.	277.91M	1.82	LYTS
Mansei Corporation	24.03M	3.14	MSPVF
Mars National Bancorp, Inc.	30.48M	3.16	MNBP
Muncy Bank Financial, Inc.	49.59M	3.54	MYBF
New ULM Telecom Inc.	36.76M	4.82	NULM
Optical Cable Corp.	15.54M	3.64	OCC
Panhandle Oil and Gas Inc.	263.49M	0.98	PHX
Park Sterling Corporation	377.26M	1.73	PSTB
Pzena Investment Management, Inc	121.26M	1.44	PZN
QAD Inc.	360.161M	1.52	QADA
Raven Industries Inc.	715.58M	2.66	RAVN
Reserve Petroleum Co.	29.42M	2.69	RSRV
Resources Connection, Inc.	551.04M	2.71	RECN
Riverview Financial Corporation	35.87M	4.63	RIVE
SBT Bancorp, Inc.	26.53M	2.89	SBTB
Servotronics Inc.	20.6182M	3.45	SVT
Shoe Carnival Inc.	492.2M	1.04	SCVL
Sierra Monitor Corp.	14.265M	2.86	SRMC
Silvercrest Asset Management Group Inc.	99.06M	3.96	SAMG
Southwest Georgia Financial Corp.	37.39M	2.68	SGB
Span-America Medical Systems Inc.	49.33M	3.6	SPAN
Stage Stores Inc.	136.97M	11.52	SSI
Stein Mart Inc.	349.6M	4.1	SMRT
Superior Industries International, Inc.	693.36M	2.66	SUP
The Farmers Bank of Appomattox	20.92M	4.15	FBPA
Unique Fabricating, Inc.	135.02M	4.43	UFAB
United Tennessee Bankshares Inc.	14.89M	2.89	UNTN
Valley Commerce Bancorp	47.59M	2.5	VCBP
VSB Bancorp, Inc.	19.36M	2.26	VSBN
Wayne Savings Bancshares Inc.	34.34M	2.88	WAYN
Wells Financial Corp.	27.8M	2.86	WEFP
Westfield Financial Inc.	131.51M	1.59	WFD
Westwood Holdings Group Inc.	486.26M	4.12	WHG
WSI Industries Inc.	8.79M	5.41	WSCI

THE TOP 100 LIST

INTERNATIONAL BUSINESS MACHINES

IBM provides information technology (IT) products and services worldwide. It creates business value for clients and solves business problems through integrated solutions that leverage information technology & knowledge of business processes.

Website: http://www.ibm.com

RANKINGS; OVERALL; #1, WITHIN TECHNOLOGY; #1

Category	Value	Ranking
Dividend Yield	3.00	78
Dividend Growth	15	70
Trailing Price/Earnings	10.4	14
S&P Financial Rating	A++	40
Beta	0.90	100
Ranking Score		**302**

Date	Yearly Dividend	Dividend Growth %	Average Dividend Yield %
2015	5.00	17	3.2
2014	4.25	23	2.7
2013	3.70	12	2.0
2012	3.30	14	1.7
2011	2.90	16	1.6
2010	2.50	16	1.7
2009	2.15	13	1.6
2008	1.90	27	2.3
2007	1.50	36	1.4
2006	1.10	41	1.1
2005	0.78	11	1.0

WALMART STORES

Wal-Mart stores Inc. operates retail stores in various formats under various banners. Its operations comprise of three reportable business segments, Walmart U.S., Walmart International and Sam's Club in three categories retail, wholesale, and others.

Website: http://www.walmart.com

RANKINGS; OVERALL; #2, WITHIN CONSUMER STAPLES; #1

Category	Value	Ranking
Dividend Yield	2.51	117
Dividend Growth	14.5	73
Trailing Price/Earnings	15.4	80
S&P Financial Rating	A++	40
Beta	0.60	25
Ranking Score		**335**

Date	Yearly Dividend	Dividend Growth %	Average Dividend Yield %
2015	1.96	2	2.8
2014	1.92	2	2.2
2013	1.88	18	2.4
2012	1.59	9	2.3
2011	1.46	20	2.4
2010	1.21	11	2.2
2009	1.09	15	2.0
2008	0.95	8	1.7
2007	0.88	31	1.9
2006	0.67	12	1.5
2005	0.60	15	1.3

McDonald's

McDonald's Corp. franchises and operates McDonald's restaurants in the food service industry. Its geographic segments include the United States, Europe, and Asia-Pacific, Middle East and Africa.

Website: http://www.mcdonalds.com

RANKINGS; OVERALL; #3, WITHIN CONSUMER DISCRETIONARY; #1

Category	Value	Ranking
Dividend Yield	3.54	49
Dividend Growth	15.5	65
Trailing Price/Earnings	19.5	133
S&P Financial Rating	A++	40
Beta	0.70	50
Ranking Score		**337**

Date	Yearly Dividend	Dividend Growth %	Average Dividend Yield %
2015	3.44	5	3.4
2014	3.28	5	3.5
2013	3.12	9	3.2
2012	2.87	13	3.3
2011	2.53	12	2.5
2010	2.26	10	2.9
2009	2.05	26	3.3
2008	1.63	9	2.6
2007	1.50	50	2.6
2006	1.00	50	2.3
2005	0.67	22	2.0

NESTLE SA ADR

Nestle SA manufactures and markets food products. The Company's product line includes milk, chocolate, confectionery, creamer, coffee, food seasoning, bottled water and pet foods among others.

Website: http://www.nestle.com

RANKINGS; OVERALL; #4, WITHIN CONSUMER STAPLES; #2

Category	Value	Ranking
Dividend Yield	2.99	80
Dividend Growth	13.5	85
Trailing Price/Earnings	17.2	103
S&P Financial Rating	A++	40
Beta	0.70	50
Ranking Score		358

Date	Yearly Dividend	Dividend Growth %	Average Dividend Yield %
2015	2.25	5	3.0
2014	2.14	5	3.3
2013	2.03	6	2.9
2012	1.91	6	3.2
2011	1.80	43	3.6
2010	1.26	-11	2.0
2009	1.41	80	2.6
2008	0.78	18	1.9
2007	0.66	12	1.2
2006	0.59	-26	1.3
2005	0.80	44	2.2

LOCKHEED MARTIN

Lockheed Martin Corp is a security and aerospace company. The Company is engaged in the research, design, development, manufacture, integration and sustainment of advanced technology systems, products and services.

Website: http://www.lockheedmartin.com

RANKINGS; OVERALL; #5, WITHIN BASIC MATERIALS; #1

Category	Value	Ranking
Dividend Yield	3.20	67
Dividend Growth	20.5	46
Trailing Price/Earnings	17.8	109
S&P Financial Rating	A++	40
Beta	0.90	100
Ranking Score		362

Date	Yearly Dividend	Dividend Growth %	Average Dividend Yield %
2015	6.15	12	3.0
2014	5.49	15	2.9
2013	4.78	15	3.2
2012	4.15	28	4.5
2011	3.25	23	4.0
2010	2.64	13	3.8
2009	2.34	28	3.1
2008	1.83	25	2.2
2007	1.47	18	1.4
2006	1.25	19	1.4
2005	1.05	15	1.7

CHEVRON CORP

Human Energy®

Chevron Corp provides administrative, financial, management and technology support to U.S. & international subsidiaries that engage in fully integrated petroleum operations, chemicals operations, mining operations, and power and energy services.

Website: http://www.chevron.com

RANKINGS; OVERALL; #6, WITHIN ENERGY; #1

Category	Value	Ranking
Dividend Yield	3.96	31
Dividend Growth	9	131
Trailing Price/Earnings	10.6	16
S&P Financial Rating	A++	40
Beta	1.1	150
Ranking Score		368

Date	Yearly Dividend	Dividend Growth %	Average Dividend Yield %
2015	4.28	2	4.4
2014	4.21	8	3.8
2013	3.90	11	3.1
2012	3.51	14	3.3
2011	3.09	9	2.9
2010	2.84	7	3.1
2009	2.66	5	3.5
2008	2.53	12	3.4
2007	2.26	12	2.4
2006	2.01	15	2.7
2005	1.75	14	3.1

VERIZON COMMUNICATIONS

Verizon Communications Inc is a provider of communications, information and entertainment products and services to consumers, businesses and governmental agencies. Its two segments are Wireless and Wireline.

Website: http://www.verizon.com

RANKINGS; OVERALL; #7, WITHIN TELECOMMUNICATIONS; #1

Category	Value	Ranking
Dividend Yield	4.39	22
Dividend Growth	3.5	195
Trailing Price/Earnings	14.2	63
S&P Financial Rating	A++	40
Beta	0.7	50
Ranking Score		370

Date	Yearly Dividend	Dividend Growth %	Average Dividend Yield %
2015	2.23	3	4.7
2014	2.16	3	4.6
2013	2.09	3	4.2
2012	2.03	3	4.7
2011	1.98	3	4.9
2010	1.93	3	5.4
2009	1.87	5	5.6
2008	1.78	7	5.2
2007	1.67	-17	3.8
2006	2.03	25	4.4
2005	1.62	17	5.3

CISCO SYSTEMS

Cisco Systems Inc. is engaged in designing, manufacturing and selling of Internet Protocol (IP) based networking products and services related to the communications and information technology (IT) industry.

Website: http://www.cisco.com

RANKINGS; OVERALL; #8, WITHIN TECHNOLOGY; #2

Category	Value	Ranking
Dividend Yield	2.91	88
Dividend Growth	22	37
Trailing Price/Earnings	14.2	56
S&P Financial Rating	A++	40
Beta	1.1	150
Ranking Score		**371**

Date	Yearly Dividend	Dividend Growth %	Average Dividend Yield %
2015	0.80	11	2.9
2014	0.72	16	2.7
2013	0.62	121	2.9
2012	0.28	133	2.2
2011	0.12	-	1.0
2010	-	-	-
2009	-	-	-
2008	-	-	-
2007	-	-	-
2006	-	-	-
2005	-	-	-

OCCIDENTAL PETROLEUM

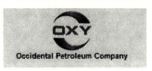

Occidental Petroleum Corp. is a multinational organization whose subsidiaries and affiliates operate in the oil and gas, chemical and midstream, marketing & other segments.

Website: http://www.oxy.com

RANKINGS; OVERALL; #9, WITHIN ENERGY; #2

Category	Value	Ranking
Dividend Yield	3.66	43
Dividend Growth	17.5	55
Trailing Price/Earnings	13.7	59
S&P Financial Rating	A++	40
Beta	1.2	175
Ranking Score		**372**

Date	Yearly Dividend	Dividend Growth %	Average Dividend Yield %
2015	2.94	2	4.0
2014	2.88	13	3.6
2013	2.56	19	2.7
2012	2.16	17	2.8
2011	1.84	25	2.0
2010	1.47	12	1.5
2009	1.31	8	1.6
2008	1.21	29	2.0
2007	0.94	18	1.2
2006	0.80	23	1.6
2005	0.65	23	1.6

TRAVELERS COMPANIES

Travelers Companies Inc through its subsidiaries provides commercial & personal property and casualty insurance products and services to businesses, government units, associations and individuals.

Website: http://www.travelers.com

RANKINGS; OVERALL; #10, WITHIN FINANCIAL; #1

Category	Value	Ranking
Dividend Yield	2.39	121
Dividend Growth	10	125
Trailing Price/Earnings	10.2	11
S&P Financial Rating	A++	40
Beta	0.8	75
Ranking Score		372

Date	Yearly Dividend	Dividend Growth %	Average Dividend Yield %
2015	2.38	11	2.3
2014	2.15	13	2.0
2013	1.96	19	2.2
2012	1.79	17	2.5
2011	1.59	25	2.7
2010	1.41	12	2.5
2009	1.23	8	2.5
2008	1.19	29	2.6
2007	1.13	18	2.1
2006	1.01	23	1.9
2005	0.91	-4	2.0

AT&T Inc

AT&T Inc. through its subsidiaries and affiliates, provides wireless and wireline telecommunications services in the United States and internationally. The Company has three reportable segments: Wireless, Wireline, and Other.

Website: http://www.att.com

RANKINGS; OVERALL; #11, WITHIN TELECOMMUNICATIONS; #2

Category	Value	Ranking
Dividend Yield	5.58	7
Dividend Growth	3	203
Trailing Price/Earnings	13.1	47
S&P Financial Rating	A++	40
Beta	0.8	75
Ranking Score		372

Date	Yearly Dividend	Dividend Growth %	Average Dividend Yield %
2015	1.88	2	5.6
2014	1.85	2	5.5
2013	1.81	2	5.1
2012	1.77	2	5.2
2011	1.73	2	5.7
2010	1.69	2	5.7
2009	1.65	3	5.9
2008	1.61	-14	5.6
2007	1.87	9	3.4
2006	1.71	32	3.7
2005	1.30	4	5.3

TEVA PHARMACEUTICAL INDUSTRIES

Teva Pharmaceutical Industries Ltd develops, manufactures, markets, and distributes generic, specialty, and other pharmaceutical products worldwide. The company operated in two segments, Generic Medicine and Specialty Medicines.

Website: http://www.tevapharm.com

RANKINGS; OVERALL; #12, WITHIN HEALTHCARE; #1

Category	Value	Ranking
Dividend Yield	2.19	143
Dividend Growth	22	38
Trailing Price/Earnings	12.3	38
S&P Financial Rating	A+	80
Beta	0.8	75
Ranking Score		**374**

Date	Yearly Dividend	Dividend Growth %	Average Dividend Yield %
2015	1.37	-	2.2
2014	1.37	7	0.6
2013	1.28	24	3.2
2012	1.03	16	2.8
2011	0.89	33	2.2
2010	0.67	40	1.3
2009	0.48	17	0.9
2008	0.41	24	1.0
2007	0.33	32	0.7
2006	0.25	14	0.8
2005	0.22	10	0.5

Qualcomm Inc

Qualcomm Inc develops digital communication technology called CDMA (Code Division Multiple Access), & owns intellectual property applicable to products that implement any version of CDMA including patents, patent applications & trade secrets.

Website: http://www.qualcomm.com

RANKINGS; OVERALL; #13, WITHIN TECHNOLOGY; #3

Category	Value	Ranking
Dividend Yield	2.81	91
Dividend Growth	15.5	68
Trailing Price/Earnings	13.4	55
S&P Financial Rating	A++	40
Beta	1.0	125
Ranking Score		**379**

Date	Yearly Dividend	Dividend Growth %	Average Dividend Yield %
2015	1.80	17	2.7
2014	1.54	28	2.2
2013	1.20	4	1.8
2012	1.15	42	1.6
2011	0.81	13	1.5
2010	0.72	9	1.5
2009	0.66	10	1.5
2008	0.60	15	1.7
2007	0.52	24	1.4
2006	0.42	31	1.2
2005	0.32	39	0.8

DEERE & COMPANY

Deer & Company operated in three business segments: agriculture/turf, construction/forestry, & financial services. The Company helps customers to be more productive as they help to improve the quality of like for people around the world.

Website: http://www.deere.com

RANKINGS; OVERALL; #14, WITHIN INDUSTRIALS; #1

Category	Value	Ranking
Dividend Yield	2.66	105
Dividend Growth	14	79
Trailing Price/Earnings	10.3	12
S&P Financial Rating	A++	40
Beta	1.1	150
Ranking Score		386

Date	Yearly Dividend	Dividend Growth %	Average Dividend Yield %
2015	2.4	8	2.7
2014	2.22	12	2.6
2013	1.99	11	2.2
2012	1.79	18	2.1
2011	1.52	31	2.0
2010	1.16	4	1.5
2009	1.12	6	2.1
2008	1.06	16	2.8
2007	0.91	17	1.0
2006	0.78	28	1.7
2005	0.61	9	0.9

EXXON MOBIL

Exxon Mobil Corporation is engaged in energy, involving exploration for, and production of, crude oil and natural transportation and sale of crude oil, natural gas and petroleum products.

Website: http://www.exxonmobil.com

RANKINGS; OVERALL; #15, WITHIN ENERGY; #3

Category	Value	Ranking
Dividend Yield	3.30	56
Dividend Growth	9	134
Trailing Price/Earnings	11.8	33
S&P Financial Rating	A++	40
Beta	1.0	125
Ranking Score		**388**

Date	Yearly Dividend	Dividend Growth %	Average Dividend Yield %
2015	2.88	7	3.5
2014	2.70	10	2.9
2013	2.46	13	2.4
2012	2.18	18	2.5
2011	1.85	6	2.2
2010	1.74	5	2.4
2009	1.66	7	2.4
2008	1.55	13	1.9
2007	1.37	7	1.5
2006	1.28	12	1.7
2005	1.14	8	2.0

INTEL CORP

Intel Corporation is a semiconductor chip maker. It develops integrated digital technology products like integrated circuits, for industries such as computing and communications.

Website: http://www.intel.com

RANKINGS; OVERALL; #16, WITHIN TECHNOLOGY; #4

Category	Value	Ranking
Dividend Yield	2.94	83
Dividend Growth	12.5	95
Trailing Price/Earnings	13.2	52
S&P Financial Rating	A++	40
Beta	1.0	125
Ranking Score		395

Date	Yearly Dividend	Dividend Growth %	Average Dividend Yield %
2015	0.96	7	3.0
2014	0.90	0	2.5
2013	0.90	3	3.5
2012	0.87	12	4.2
2011	0.78	24	3.2
2010	0.63	13	3.0
2009	0.56	2	2.8
2008	0.55	22	3.7
2007	0.45	13	1.7
2006	0.40	25	2.0
2005	0.32	100	1.3

AMGEN INC

Amgen Inc is a biotechnology company that discovers, develops, manufactures and delivers human therapeutics. It focuses for the treatment of illness in the areas of oncology, hematology, inflammation, bone health, nephrology, cardiovascular, and general medicine.

Website: http://www.amgen.com

RANKINGS; OVERALL; #17, WITHIN HEALTHCARE; #2

Category	Value	Ranking
Dividend Yield	1.98	157
Dividend Growth	30	18
Trailing Price/Earnings	18.2	114
S&P Financial Rating	A++	40
Beta	0.8	75
Ranking Score		**404**

Date	Yearly Dividend	Dividend Growth %	Average Dividend Yield %
2015	3.16	30	2.0
2014	2.44	30	1.5
2013	1.88	31	1.7
2012	1.44	157	1.7
2011	0.56	-	0.90
2010	-	-	-
2009	-	-	-
2008	-	-	-
2007	-	-	-
2006	-	-	-
2005	-	-	-

PROCTER & GAMBLE CO

Procter & Gamble Co provides branded consumer packaged goods. It markets its products in about 180 countries through mass merchandisers, grocery stores, membership club stores, drug stores, department stores among others.

Website: http://www.pg.com

RANKINGS; OVERALL; #18, WITHIN CONSUMER STAPLES; #3

Category	Value	Ranking
Dividend Yield	3.31	55
Dividend Growth	9.5	129
Trailing Price/Earnings	20.2	141
S&P Financial Rating	A++	40
Beta	0.7	50
Ranking Score		**415**

Date	Yearly Dividend	Dividend Growth %	Average Dividend Yield %
2015	2.59	6	3.1
2014	2.45	16	2.8
2013	2.29	7	2.9
2012	2.14	9	3.3
2011	1.97	9	3.1
2010	1.80	10	2.9
2009	1.64	13	2.8
2008	1.45	13	2.5
2007	1.28	11	1.9
2006	1.15	12	1.9
2005	1.03	5	1.9

DUKE ENERGY

Duke Energy Corporation operated as an energy company. The Company operates in three business segments; Regulated Utilities, International Energy and Commercial Power.

Website: http://www.duke-energy.com

RANKINGS; OVERALL; #19, WITHIN UTILITIES; #1

Category	Value	Ranking
Dividend Yield	4.17	25
Dividend Growth	11.5	104
Trailing Price/Earnings	20.3	142
S&P Financial Rating	A	120
Beta	0.6	25
Ranking Score		**417**

Date	Yearly Dividend	Dividend Growth %	Average Dividend Yield %
2015	3.24	3	4.3
2014	3.15	2	3.8
2013	3.09	2	4.5
2012	3.03	2	4.8
2011	2.97	2	4.5
2010	2.91	3	5.5
2009	2.82	4	5.5
2008	2.70	5	6.0
2007	2.58	-32	4.3
2006	3.78	8	3.8
2005	3.51	13	4.3

RAYTHEON CO

Raytheon

Raytheon Co together with its subsidiaries is engaged in developing integrated defense systems. The Company offers air and missile defense; radar solutions; naval combat and ship electronic systems; command, control and communications systems.

Website: http://www.raytheon.com

RANKINGS; OVERALL; #20, WITHIN INDUSTRIALS; #2

Category	Value	Ranking
Dividend Yield	2.55	113
Dividend Growth	14	81
Trailing Price/Earnings	15.5	83
S&P Financial Rating	A++	40
Beta	0.9	100
Ranking Score		**417**

Date	Yearly Dividend	Dividend Growth %	Average Dividend Yield %
2015	2.68	11	2.5
2014	2.42	10	2.2
2013	2.20	10	2.4
2012	2.00	16	3.5
2011	1.72	15	3.6
2010	1.50	21	3.1
2009	1.24	11	2.4
2008	1.12	10	2.2
2007	1.02	6	1.7
2006	0.96	9	1.8
2005	0.88	10	2.2

BANK OF NOVA SCOTIA

Bank of Nova Scotia is a diversified financial services institution that provides financial products and services to retail, commercial and corporate customers around the world.

Website: http://www.scotiabank.com

RANKINGS; OVERALL; #21, WITHIN FINANCIAL; #2

Category	Value	Ranking
Dividend Yield	4.09	29
Dividend Growth	5	177
Trailing Price/Earnings	11.3	22
S&P Financial Rating	A	120
Beta	0.8	75
Ranking Score		423

Date	Yearly Dividend	Dividend Growth %	Average Dividend Yield %
2015	2.72	6	4.3
2014	2.56	7	3.9
2013	2.39	9	3.6
2012	2.19	7	3.9
2011	2.05	5	4.1
2010	1.96	0	3.4
2009	1.96	2	4.0
2008	1.92	10	5.8
2007	1.74	16	3.6
2006	1.50	14	3.0
2005	1.32	25	3.0

JOHNSON & JOHNSON

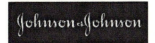

Johnson & Johnson is engaged in the research & development, manufacture, and sale of a broad range of products in the healthcare field. It has three business segments: Consumer, Pharmaceutical, and Medical Devices & Diagnostics.

Website: http://www.jnj.com

RANKINGS; OVERALL; #22, WITHIN HEALTHCARE; #3

Category	Value	Ranking
Dividend Yield	3.02	77
Dividend Growth	8.5	137
Trailing Price/Earnings	16.8	96
S&P Financial Rating	A++	40
Beta	0.80	75
Ranking Score		425

Date	Yearly Dividend	Dividend Growth %	Average Dividend Yield %
2015	2.95	7	3.0
2014	2.76	6	2.7
2013	2.59	8	3
2012	2.40	7	3.6
2011	2.25	6	3.5
2010	2.11	10	3.4
2009	1.93	7	3.3
2008	1.80	11	2.8
2007	1.62	11	2.5
2006	1.46	14	2.3
2005	1.28	16	2.0

CocaCola

Coca-Cola Co manufactures, distributes and markets non-alcoholic beverage concentrates and syrups. The company primarily offers sparkling beverages and still beverages.

Website: http://www.cocacola.com

RANKINGS; OVERALL; #23, WITHIN CONSUMER STAPLES; #4

Category	Value	Ranking
Dividend Yield	3.24	61
Dividend Growth	8.5	138
Trailing Price/Earnings	19.9	139
S&P Financial Rating	A++	40
Beta	0.7	50
Ranking Score		428

Date	Yearly Dividend	Dividend Growth %	Average Dividend Yield %
2015	1.32	8	3.2
2014	1.22	9	2.9
2013	1.12	10	2.7
2012	1.02	8	2.8
2011	0.94	7	2.7
2010	0.88	7	2.7
2009	0.82	8	2.9
2008	0.76	12	3.4
2007	0.68	10	2.2
2006	0.62	11	2.6
2005	0.56	12	2.8

Total SA ADR

Total SA is an integrated oil and gas company. It explores and develops oil and gas properties, liquefied natural gas, petrochemicals and specialty chemicals. It is also engaged in trading and shipping of crude oil and petroleum products.

Website: http://www.total.com

RANKINGS; OVERALL; #24, WITHIN ENERGY; #4

Category	Value	Ranking
Dividend Yield	5.68	6
Dividend Growth	2.5	211
Trailing Price/Earnings	9.5	5
S&P Financial Rating	A++	40
Beta	1.2	175
Ranking Score		**437**

Date	Yearly Dividend	Dividend Growth %	Average Dividend Yield %
2015	2.73	-14	5.5
2014	3.17	-0.3	6.2
2013	3.18	7	5.2
2012	2.96	-5	5.7
2011	3.11	23	6.1
2010	2.53	-23	4.7
2009	3.28	6	5.1
2008	3.10	10	5.6
2007	2.81	31	3.4
2006	2.15	14	3.0
2005	1.88	-17	3.0

Microsoft Corp is engaged in designing, manufacturing, selling devices, and online advertising to a global customer audience. Its products include operating systems for computing devices, servers, phones, and other intelligent devices.

Website: http://www.microsoft.com

RANKINGS; OVERALL; #25, WITHIN TECHNOLOGY; #5

Category	Value	Ranking
Dividend Yield	2.61	109
Dividend Growth	2.5	67
Trailing Price/Earnings	15.5	97
S&P Financial Rating	A++	40
Beta	1.0	125
Ranking Score		438

Date	Yearly Dividend	Dividend Growth %	Average Dividend Yield %
2015	1.24	16	2.7
2014	1.07	20	2.5
2013	0.89	17	2.6
2012	0.76	25	3.1
2011	0.61	17	2.6
2010	0.52	4	2.0
2009	0.50	16	1.7
2008	0.43	10	2.4
2007	0.39	15	1.2
2006	0.34	6	1.2
2005	0.32	0	1.2

CHUBB CORP

**CHUBB GROUP
OF INSURANCE COMPANIES**

Chubb Corp is a holding company. The Company, through its subsidiaries is engaged in property and casualty insurance to business and individuals.

Website: http://www.chubb.com

RANKINGS; OVERALL; #26, WITHIN FINANCIAL; #3

Category	Value	Ranking
Dividend Yield	2.29	131
Dividend Growth	7.5	149
Trailing Price/Earnings	13.2	50
S&P Financial Rating	A++	40
Beta	0.8	75
Ranking Score		**445**

Date	Yearly Dividend	Dividend Growth %	Average Dividend Yield %
2015	2.64	32	2.4
2014	2.00	14	1.9
2013	1.76	7	1.8
2012	1.64	6	2.2
2011	1.54	4	2.3
2010	1.48	6	2.5
2009	1.40	6	2.9
2008	1.32	14	2.6
2007	1.16	16	2.1
2006	1.00	16	1.9
2005	0.86	10	1.8

ACCENTURE PLC

Accenture PLC is a professional service company. The Company is engaged in providing management consulting, technology and outsourcing services to clients.

Website: http://www.accenture.com

RANKINGS; OVERALL; #27, WITHIN TECHNOLOGY; #6

Category	Value	Ranking
Dividend Yield	2.18	144
Dividend Growth	30.5	15
Trailing Price/Earnings	18.9	125
S&P Financial Rating	A++	40
Beta	1.0	125
Ranking Score		449

Date	Yearly Dividend	Dividend Growth %	Average Dividend Yield %
2015	2.04	10	2.3
2014	1.86	15	2.2
2013	1.62	20	2.1
2012	1.35	50	2.2
2011	0.90	-20	2.1
2010	1.13	126	1.7
2009	0.50	19	1.8
2008	0.42	20	1.5
2007	0.35	17	1.2
2006	0.30	-	1.0
2005	-	-	1.0

GENERAL MILLS

GENERAL MILLS

General Mills Inc is a manufacturer and marketer of branded customer foods sold through retail stores. It supplies branded and unbranded food products to the foodservice and commercial baking industries.

Website: http://www.generalmills.com

RANKINGS; OVERALL; #28, WITHIN CONSUMER STAPLES; #5

Category	Value	Ranking
Dividend Yield	3.16	68
Dividend Growth	11.5	105
Trailing Price/Earnings	20.5	146
S&P Financial Rating	A+	80
Beta	0.7	50
Ranking Score		449

Date	Yearly Dividend	Dividend Growth %	Average Dividend Yield %
2015	1.67	8	3.1
2014	1.55	17	3.0
2013	1.32	7	2.9
2012	1.22	9	3.1
2011	1.12	17	2.9
2010	0.96	12	3.0
2009	0.86	9	2.5
2008	0.79	10	2.7
2007	0.72	7	2.7
2006	0.67	8	2.4
2005	0.62	5	2.6

SOUTHERN CO.

The Southern Company together with its subsidiaries, operates as a public electric utility company. It is involved in the generation, transmission, and distribution of electricity through coal, nuclear, oil and gas, and hydro resources in the states of Alabama, Georgia, Florida, and Mississippi.

Website: http://www.southernco.com

RANKINGS; OVERALL; #29, WITHIN UTILITIES; #2

Category	Value	Ranking
Dividend Yield	4.90	10
Dividend Growth	4	188
Trailing Price/Earnings	17.3	106
S&P Financial Rating	A	120
Beta	0.6	25
Ranking Score		**449**

Date	Yearly Dividend	Dividend Growth %	Average Dividend Yield %
2015	2.15	3	4.8
2014	2.08	17	4.2
2013	2.01	7	4.9
2012	1.94	9	4.5
2011	1.87	17	4.1
2010	1.80	12	4.7
2009	1.73	9	5.2
2008	1.66	10	4.5
2007	1.60	7	4.1
2006	1.54	4	4.2
2005	1.48	4	4.3

TorontoDominion Bank

Toronto-Dominion Bank is a Canadian bank. Together with its subsidiaries, it provides financial and banking services in North America and internationally. The company operates through Canadian Retail, U.S. Retail, and Wholesale Banking segments.

Website: http://www.td.com

RANKINGS; OVERALL; #30, WITHIN FINANCIAL; #4

Category	Value	Ranking
Dividend Yield	3.67	41
Dividend Growth	7.5	157
Trailing Price/Earnings	12.8	43
S&P Financial Rating	B++	160
Beta	0.7	50
Ranking Score		451

Date	Yearly Dividend	Dividend Growth %	Average Dividend Yield %
2015	2.00	9	3.7
2014	1.84	14	3.5
2013	1.62	12	3.4
2012	1.45	11	3.4
2011	1.31	7	3.6
2010	1.22	0	3.2
2009	1.22	3	3.4
2008	1.18	10	6.3
2007	1.07	20	2.8
2006	0.89	14	2.6
2005	0.78	11	2.6

ANHEUSERBUSCH INBEV SA

Anheuser-Busch Inbev SA, a brewing company, engages in the production, distribution, and sale of beer, alcoholic beverages, and soft drinks worldwide. It offers a portfolio of approximately 200 beer brands, which includes Budweiser, Corona and Stella Artois.

Website: http://www.ab-inbev.com

RANKINGS; OVERALL; #31, WITHIN CONSUMER STAPLES; #6

Category	Value	Ranking
Dividend Yield	2.91	87
Dividend Growth	22.7	35
Trailing Price/Earnings	22.2	166
S&P Financial Rating	A++	40
Beta	1.0	125
Ranking Score		**453**

Date	Yearly Dividend	Dividend Growth %	Average Dividend Yield %
2015	3.95	22	3.3
2014	3.25	7	2.9
2013	3.03	93	2.8
2012	1.57	33	1.8
2011	1.18	141	1.9
2010	0.49	-	0.9
2009	-	-	-
2008	-	-	-
2007	-	-	-
2006	-	-	-
2005	-	-	-

MARATHON PETROLEUM

Marathon Petroleum Corp is a supplier of gasoline and distillates to resellers and consumers. Its refining, marketing and transportation operations are concentrated in the Midwest, Gulf Coast and Southeast regions of the U.S.

Website: http://www.marathonpetroleum.com

RANKINGS; OVERALL; #32, WITHIN ENERGY; #5

Category	Value	Ranking
Dividend Yield	1.96	159
Dividend Growth	60	6
Trailing Price / Earnings	11.9	35
S&P Financial Rating	A+	80
Beta	1.2	175
Ranking Score		**455**

Date	Yearly Dividend	Dividend Growth %	Average Dividend Yield %
2015	1.14	24	2.3
2014	0.92	19	2.1
2013	0.77	28	2.0
2012	0.60	160	1.6
2011	0.23	-	1.3
2010	-	-	-
2009	-	-	-
2008	-	-	-
2007	-	-	-
2006	-	-	-
2005	-	-	-

ORACLE CORPORATION

Oracle Corporation develops, manufactures, markets, hosts and supports database and middleware software, application software, cloud infrastructure, hardware system including computer server, storage and networking products and related services.

Website: http://www.oracle.com

RANKINGS; OVERALL; #33, WITHIN TECHNOLOGY; #7

Category	Value	Ranking
Dividend Yield	1.37	195
Dividend Growth	83	2
Trailing Price/Earnings	14.8	72
S&P Financial Rating	A++	40
Beta	1.1	150
Ranking Score		455

Date	Yearly Dividend	Dividend Growth %	Average Dividend Yield %
2015	0.51	6	1.2
2014	0.48	300	1.1
2013	0.12	-50	0.60
2012	0.24	14	0.70
2011	0.21	5	0.90
2010	0.20	300	0.60
2009	0.05	-	0.60
2008	-	-	-
2007	-	-	-
2006	-	-	-
2005	-	-	-

ROYAL DUTCH SHELL PLC

Royal Dutch Shell PLC is an integrated oil & gas company. The Company explores for and extracts crude oil, natural gas and natural gas liquids. It also liquefies and transports gas.

Website: http://www.shell.com

RANKINGS; OVERALL; #34, WITHIN BASIC MATERIALS; #2

Category	Value	Ranking
Dividend Yield	5.84	3
Dividend Growth	3	201
Trailing Price/Earnings	14.4	68
S&P Financial Rating	A++	40
Beta	1.1	150
Ranking Score		**462**

Date	Yearly Dividend	Dividend Growth %	Average Dividend Yield %
2015	3.76	1	6.5
2014	3.72	4	5.4
2013	3.56	4	4.7
2012	3.42	2	4.8
2011	3.36	0	4.4
2010	3.36	1	5.0
2009	3.32	6	5.7
2008	3.12	11	6.1
2007	2.81	49	3.4
2006	1.89	-	2.7
2005	-	-	-

DISCOVER®

Discover Financial Services is a direct banking and payment services company. The Company offers credit card loans, private student loans, personal loans, home equity loans and deposits products.

Website: http://www.discoverfinancial.com

RANKINGS; OVERALL; #35, WITHIN FINANCIAL; #5

Category	Value	Ranking
Dividend Yield	1.91	165
Dividend Growth	30.5	16
Trailing Price/Earnings	10.8	18
S&P Financial Rating	A	120
Beta	1.1	150
Ranking Score		469

Date	Yearly Dividend	Dividend Growth %	Average Dividend Yield %
2015	1.08	17	1.9
2014	0.92	53	1.4
2013	0.60	50	1.3
2012	0.40	100	1.1
2011	0.20	150	1.2
2010	0.08	-22	0.4
2009	0.12	-50	0.5
2008	0.24	300	2.5
2007	0.06	-	0.8
2006	-	-	-
2005	-	-	-

EMERSON ELECTRIC CO

Emerson Electric Co is engaged in designing and supplying products and technology, and delivering engineering services and solutions in industrial, commercial and consumer markets.

Website: http://www.emerson.com

RANKINGS; OVERALL; #36, WITHIN INDUSTRIALS; #3

Category	Value	Ranking
Dividend Yield	3.22	64
Dividend Growth	8	145
Trailing Price/Earnings	14.8	71
S&P Financial Rating	A++	40
Beta	1.1	150
Ranking Score		470

Date	Yearly Dividend	Dividend Growth %	Average Dividend Yield %
2015	1.88	9	3.3
2014	1.72	5	2.9
2013	1.64	3	2.4
2012	1.60	16	3.0
2011	1.38	3	3.1
2010	1.34	2	2.4
2009	1.32	10	3.1
2008	1.20	14	3.4
2007	1.05	18	1.9
2006	0.89	7	2.1
2005	0.83	2	2.3

ConocoPhillips

ConocoPhillips is engaged in exploration, development and production of crude oil and natural gas.

Website: http://www.conocophillips.com

RANKINGS; OVERALL; #37, WITHIN ENERGY; #6

Category	Value	Ranking
Dividend Yield	4.35	23
Dividend Growth	8.5	135
Trailing Price/Earnings	13.6	58
S&P Financial Rating	A+	80
Beta	1.2	175
Ranking Score		**471**

Date	Yearly Dividend	Dividend Growth %	Average Dividend Yield %
2015	2.94	4	5.1
2014	2.84	5	4.1
2013	2.70	3	3.8
2012	2.64	16	4.6
2011	2.64	3	3.6
2010	2.15	2	3.2
2009	1.91	10	3.7
2008	1.88	14	3.6
2007	1.64	18	1.9
2006	1.44	7	2.0
2005	1.18	16	2.0

AMERICAN ELECTRIC POWER CO.

American Electric Power Co. Inc. is a public utility holding company, through its subsidiaries, provides electric service, consisting of generation, transmission and distribution, on an integrated basis to its retail customers.

Website: http://www.aep.com

RANKINGS; OVERALL; #38, WITHIN UTILITIES; #3

Category	Value	Ranking
Dividend Yield	3.79	35
Dividend Growth	4	185
Trailing Price/Earnings	16.1	89
S&P Financial Rating	A	120
Beta	0.7	50
Ranking Score		479

Date	Yearly Dividend	Dividend Growth %	Average Dividend Yield %
2015	2.15	6	3.8
2014	2.03	4	3.3
2013	1.95	4	4.2
2012	1.88	2	4.4
2011	1.85	8	4.5
2010	1.71	4	4.8
2009	1.64	0	4.7
2008	1.64	4	4.9
2007	1.58	5	3.4
2006	1.50	6	3.5
2005	1.42	1	3.8

UNITEDHEALTH GROUP INC.

UNITEDHEALTH GROUP®

UnitedHealth Group Inc. designs products, provides services and applies technologies that improve access to health and well-being services, simplify the health care experience and make health care more affordable.

Website: http://www.unitedhealthgroup.com

RANKINGS; OVERALL; #39, WITHIN HEALTHCARE; #4

Category	Value	Ranking
Dividend Yield	1.32	202
Dividend Growth	94	1
Trailing Price/Earnings	19.8	138
S&P Financial Rating	A++	40
Beta	0.9	100
Ranking Score		481

Date	Yearly Dividend	Dividend Growth %	Average Dividend Yield %
2015	1.88	33	1.6
2014	1.41	34	1.4
2013	1.05	31	1.4
2012	0.80	31	1.5
2011	0.61	49	1.2
2010	0.41	1266	1.1
2009	0.03	0	0.1
2008	0.03	0	0.1
2007	0.03	0	0.1
2006	0.03	50	0.1
2005	0.02	0	0

GlaxoSmithKline PLC ADR.

GlaxoSmithKline PLC creates, discovers, develops, manufactures and markets pharmaceutical products including vaccines, over-the-counter (OTC) medicines and health-related consumer products.

Website: http://www.gsk.com

RANKINGS; OVERALL; #40, WITHIN HEALTHCARE; #5

Category	Value	Ranking
Dividend Yield	5.69	5
Dividend Growth	3	199
Trailing Price/Earnings	19	126
S&P Financial Rating	A+	80
Beta	0.8	75
Ranking Score		**485**

Date	Yearly Dividend	Dividend Growth %	Average Dividend Yield %
2015	2.48	-6	5.7
2014	2.65	10	6.2
2013	2.41	-3	4.5
2012	2.48	12	5.3
2011	2.21	11	4.8
2010	2.00	8	5.1
2009	1.86	-13	4.4
2008	2.14	4	5.7
2007	2.06	18	4.1
2006	1.74	14	3.3
2005	1.53	-4	3.0

RIO TINTO PLC ADR

RioTinto

Rio Tinto PLC is an international mining group engaged in finding, mining and processing the Earth's mineral resources. Its main products are Bauxite, Alumina, Copper, Gold, Molybdenum, Silver, Nickel, Diamonds and Rutile.

Website: http://www.riotinto.com

RANKINGS; OVERALL; #41, WITHIN BASIC MATERIALS; #3

Category	Value	Ranking
Dividend Yield	4.55	17
Dividend Growth	10	123
Trailing Price/Earnings	8.4	2
S&P Financial Rating	A	120
Beta	1.4	225
Ranking Score		**487**

Date	Yearly Dividend	Dividend Growth %	Average Dividend Yield %
2015	2.21	9	5.5
2014	2.03	15	4.4
2013	1.76	7	3.1
2012	1.64	40	2.8
2011	1.17	33	2.4
2010	0.88	30	1.2
2009	0.68	-55	1.3
2008	1.52	31	6.8
2007	1.16	41	1.1
2006	0.82	-2	1.5
2005	0.84	281	1.8

BANK OF MONTREAL

Bank of Montreal is a financial services provider based in North America. It provides retail banking, wealth management and investment banking products & services.

Website: http://www.bmo.com

RANKINGS; OVERALL; #42, WITHIN FINANCIAL; #6

Category	Value	Ranking
Dividend Yield	4.10	28
Dividend Growth	1	217
Trailing Price/Earnings	11.9	34
S&P Financial Rating	B++	160
Beta	0.7	50
Ranking Score		**489**

Date	Yearly Dividend	Dividend Growth %	Average Dividend Yield %
2015	3.24	5	4.2
2014	3.08	5	3.9
2013	2.94	4	4.2
2012	2.82	0	4.6
2011	2.80	0	5.1
2010	2.80	0	4.7
2009	2.80	0	4.7
2008	2.80	4	10.2
2007	2.70	19	4.5
2006	2.26	22	3.4
2005	1.85	13	2.7

PUBLIC STORAGE

Public Storage is engaged in the acquisition, development, ownership and operation of self-storage facilities which offers storage spaces for lease, generally on a month-to-month basis, for personal and business use.

Website: http://www.publicstorage.com

RANKINGS; OVERALL; #43, WITHIN
REAL ESTATE INVESTMENT; #1

Category	Value	Ranking
Dividend Yield	3.63	47
Dividend Growth	18	53
Trailing Price/Earnings	37.9	236
S&P Financial Rating	A+	80
Beta	0.8	75
Ranking Score		491

Date	Yearly Dividend	Dividend Growth %	Average Dividend Yield %
2015	6.50	16	3.1
2014	5.60	9	3.0
2013	5.15	17	3.4
2012	4.40	21	3.0
2011	3.65	20	2.7
2010	3.05	39	3.0
2009	2.20	0	2.7
2008	2.20	10	2.8
2007	2.00	0	2.7
2006	2.00	5	2.1
2005	1.90	6	2.8

KIMBERLYCLARK CORP.

✿ Kimberly-Clark

Kimberly-Clark Corp. is engaged in the manufacturing and marketing of products made from natural or synthetic fibers using technologies in fibers, nonwovens and absorbency.

Website: http://www.kimberly-clark.com

RANKINGS; OVERALL; #44, WITHIN CONSUMER STAPLES; #7

Category	Value	Ranking
Dividend Yield	3.22	65
Dividend Growth	7.5	154
Trailing Price/Earnings	27.1	211
S&P Financial Rating	A++	40
Beta	0.6	25
Ranking Score		495

Date	Yearly Dividend	Dividend Growth %	Average Dividend Yield %
2015	3.52	5	3.1
2014	3.36	4	2.9
2013	3.24	9	3.1
2012	2.96	6	3.5
2011	2.80	6	3.8
2010	2.64	10	4.2
2009	2.40	3	3.8
2008	2.32	9	4.4
2007	2.12	8	3.1
2006	1.96	9	2.9
2005	1.80	17	3.0

PPL Corp.

PPL Corp. is an energy and utility holding company through its subsidiaries, is engaged in the generation and marketing of electricity in the northeastern and western U.S. and in the delivery of electricity in Pennsylvania and the U.K.

Website: http://www.pplweb.com

RANKINGS; OVERALL; #45, WITHIN UTILITIES; #4

Category	Value	Ranking
Dividend Yield	4.42	20
Dividend Growth	3.5	194
Trailing Price/Earnings	14.8	73
S&P Financial Rating	B++	160
Beta	0.7	50
Ranking Score		497

Date	Yearly Dividend	Dividend Growth %	Average Dividend Yield %
2015	1.50	1	4.5
2014	1.49	1	4.1
2013	1.47	2	4.9
2012	1.44	3	5.0
2011	1.40	0	4.8
2010	1.40	1	5.3
2009	1.38	3	4.3
2008	1.34	10	4.4
2007	1.22	11	2.3
2006	1.10	30	3.1
2005	0.85	4	3.3

TARGET CORP.

Target Corporation operates as a general merchandise retailer in the United States and Canada. It offers household essentials, including pharmacy, beauty, personal care, baby care, cleaning, and paper products; music, movies, books, computer software, sporting goods, and toys; electronics, such as video game hardware and software; and apparel for women, men, boys, girls, toddlers, infants, and newborns, as well as intimate apparel, jewelry, accessories, and shoes.

Website: http://www.targetcorp.com

RANKINGS; OVERALL; #46, WITHIN CONSUMER STAPLES; #8

Category	Value	Ranking
Dividend Yield	2.63	108
Dividend Growth	21	43
Trailing Price/Earnings	23.2	179
S&P Financial Rating	A	120
Beta	0.70	50
Ranking Score		500

Date	Yearly Dividend	Dividend Growth %	Average Dividend Yield %
2015	2.16	14	2.8
2014	1.90	20	2.5
2013	1.58	20	2.5
2012	1.32	20	2.2
2011	1.10	31	2.2
2010	0.84	27	1.4
2009	0.66	10	1.4
2008	0.60	15	1.7
2007	0.52	18	1.0
2006	0.44	22	0.8
2005	0.36	20	0.7

UNILEVER PLC.

Unilever

Unilever PLC operates in the fast-moving consumer goods market in the Americas, Europe, Asia, Australasia, Africa, the Middle East, Turkey, the Russian Federation, Ukraine, and Belarus. The company operates through Personal Care, Foods, Refreshment, and Home Care segments.

Website: http://www.unilever.co.uk

RANKINGS; OVERALL; #47, WITHIN CONSUMER STAPLES; #9

Category	Value	Ranking
Dividend Yield	3.25	60
Dividend Growth	6.5	166
Trailing Price/Earnings	19.8	137
S&P Financial Rating	A++	40
Beta	0.90	100
Ranking Score		503

Date	Yearly Dividend	Dividend Growth %	Average Dividend Yield %
2015	1.32	13	3.1
2014	1.51	8	3.7
2013	1.40	14	3.4
2012	1.23	-1	3.2
2011	1.24	11	3.7
2010	1.12	12	3.6
2009	1.00	-	3.2
2008	1.00	1	4.3
2007	0.99	-17	2.6
2006	1.19	49	2.1
2005	0.80	7	2.0

MERCK & CO. INC.

Merck & Co., Inc. provides health care solutions worldwide. The company offer therapeutic and preventive agents to treat cardiovascular, type 2 diabetes, asthma, nasal allergy symptoms, allergic rhinitis, chronic hepatitis C virus, HIV-1 infection, fungal infections, intra-abdominal infections, hypertension, arthritis and pain, inflammatory, osteoporosis, male pattern hair loss, and fertility diseases.

Website: http://www.merck.com

RANKINGS; OVERALL; #48, WITHIN HEALTHCARE; #6

Category	Value	Ranking
Dividend Yield	2.98	81
Dividend Growth	1.5	215
Trailing Price/Earnings	16.7	94
S&P Financial Rating	A++	40
Beta	0.80	75
Ranking Score		**505**

Date	Yearly Dividend	Dividend Growth %	Average Dividend Yield %
2015	1.80	2	3.2
2014	1.77	2	3.1
2013	1.73	2	3.5
2012	1.69	8	4.1
2011	1.56	3	4.1
2010	1.52	-	4.2
2009	1.52	-	4.2
2008	1.52	-	5.0
2007	1.52	-	2.6
2006	1.52	-	3.5
2005	1.52	1	4.8

NOVARTIS AG

℧ NOVARTIS

Novartis AG researches, develops, manufactures, and markets a range of health-care products worldwide. Its Pharmaceuticals division offers patented prescription medicines in various therapeutic areas, such as oncology, cardio-metabolic, immunology and dermatology, retina, respiratory, neuroscience, and established medicines.

Website: http://www.novartis.com

RANKINGS; OVERALL; #49, WITHIN HEALTHCARE; #7

Category	Value	Ranking
Dividend Yield	2.61	110
Dividend Growth	12.5	98
Trailing Price/Earnings	23.7	183
S&P Financial Rating	A++	40
Beta	0.80	75
Ranking Score		506

Date	Yearly Dividend	Dividend Growth %	Average Dividend Yield %
2015	2.66	2	2.7
2014	2.72	8	2.9
2013	2.53	2	3.2
2012	2.48	5	3.9
2011	2.36	21	4.1
2010	1.95	14	3.3
2009	1.71	11	3.2
2008	1.54	40	3.1
2007	1.10	24	2.0
2006	0.89	3	1.6
2005	0.86	6	1.7

KELLOGG COMPANY

Kellogg Company, together with its subsidiaries, manufactures and markets ready-to-eat cereal and convenience foods. The company operates through U.S. Morning Foods, U.S. Snacks, U.S. Specialty, North America Other, Europe, Latin America, and Asia Pacific segments. Its principal products include ready-to-eat cereals and convenience foods, such as cookies, crackers, savory snacks, frozen foods, toaster pastries, cereal bars, fruit-flavored snacks, frozen waffles, and veggie foods, as well as health and wellness business bars, and beverages.

Website: http://www.kelloggcompany.com

RANKINGS; OVERALL; #50, WITHIN CONSUMER STAPLES; #10

Category	Value	Ranking
Dividend Yield	3.10	71
Dividend Growth	6.5	165
Trailing Price/Earnings	16.9	100
S&P Financial Rating	A	120
Beta	0.70	50
Ranking Score		506

Date	Yearly Dividend	Dividend Growth %	Average Dividend Yield %
2015	1.98	4	3.0
2014	1.90	6	2.9
2013	1.80	3	3.0
2012	1.74	4	3.1
2011	1.67	7	3.3
2010	1.56	9	3.1
2009	1.43	10	2.7
2008	1.30	8	3.0
2007	1.20	5	2.3
2006	1.14	8	2.3
2005	1.06	5	2.5

SIEMENS

Siemens Aktiengesellschaft operates as a technology company worldwide. The company's Power and Gas segment offers gas and steam turbines, generators, compressors, power plant solutions, and instrumentation and control systems for generating electricity, and producing and transporting oil and gas.

Website: http://www.siemens.com

RANKINGS; OVERALL; #51, WITHIN INDUSTRIALS; #4

Category	Value	Ranking
Dividend Yield	3.49	50
Dividend Growth	14.5	72
Trailing Price/Earnings	14.3	65
S&P Financial Rating	A	120
Beta	1.3	200
Ranking Score		507

Date	Yearly Dividend	Dividend Growth %	Average Dividend Yield %
2015	3.96	32	3.7
2014	3.00	2	3.6
2013	2.95	-0.3	2.9
2012	2.96	8	3.6
2011	2.74	132	3.9
2010	1.18	-1	1.3
2009	1.19	25	1.7
2008	1.58	10	3.1
2007	1.44	12	1.2
2006	1.29	32	1.6
2005	0.98	-	1.5

PRUDENTIAL FINANCIAL INC.

Prudential Financial, Inc. provides insurance, investment management, and other financial products and services to individual and institutional customers in the United States and internationally. The company principally offers life insurance, annuities, retirement-related services, mutual funds, and investment management products.

Website: http://www.prudential.com

RANKINGS; OVERALL; #52, WITHIN FINANCIAL; #7

Category	Value	Ranking
Dividend Yield	2.78	96
Dividend Growth	17.5	56
Trailing Price/Earnings	8.2	1
S&P Financial Rating	B++	160
Beta	1.3	200
Ranking Score		513

Date	Yearly Dividend	Dividend Growth %	Average Dividend Yield %
2015	2.44	12	2.9
2014	2.17	25	2.4
2013	1.73	8	1.9
2012	1.60	10	3.0
2011	1.45	26	2.9
2010	1.15	64	2.0
2009	0.70	21	1.4
2008	0.58	-50	1.9
2007	1.15	21	1.2
2006	0.95	22	1.1
2005	0.78	24	1.1

THE TJX COMPANY, INC.

The TJX Companies, Inc. operates as an off-price apparel and home fashions retailer in the United States and internationally. It operates through four segments: Marmaxx, HomeGoods, TJX Canada, and TJX Europe. The company sells family apparel, including footwear and accessories; home fashions, such as home basics, accent furniture, lamps, rugs, wall décor, decorative accessories, and giftware; and other merchandise.

Website: http://www.tjx.com

RANKINGS; OVERALL; #53, WITHIN CONSUMER DISCRETIONARY; #2

Category	Value	Ranking
Dividend Yield	1.28	207
Dividend Growth	21.5	40
Trailing Price/Earnings	21	152
S&P Financial Rating	A++	40
Beta	0.80	75
Ranking Score		514

Date	Yearly Dividend	Dividend Growth %	Average Dividend Yield %
2015	0.84	25	1.2
2014	0.67	22	1.0
2013	0.55	57	0.9
2012	0.35	-24	1.0
2011	0.46	59	1.1
2010	0.29	21	1.3
2009	0.24	41	1.3
2008	0.17	-5	2.0
2007	0.18	29	1.2
2006	0.14	-	1.0
2005	0.14	75	1.0

UNION PACIFIC CORPORATION

Union Pacific Corporation, through its subsidiary, Union Pacific Railroad Company, operates railroads in the United States. The company offers freight transportation services for agricultural products, including grains, commodities produced from grains, and food and beverage products; automotive products, such as finished vehicles and automotive parts; and chemicals consisting of industrial chemicals, plastics, crude oil, liquid petroleum gases, fertilizers, soda ash, sodium products, and phosphorus rock and sulfur products.

Website: http://www.up.com

RANKINGS; OVERALL; #54, WITHIN INDUSTRIALS; #5

Category	Value	Ranking
Dividend Yield	2.08	148
Dividend Growth	28	22
Trailing Price/Earnings	21.3	157
S&P Financial Rating	A++	40
Beta	1.1	150
Ranking Score		517

Date	Yearly Dividend	Dividend Growth %	Average Dividend Yield %
2015	2.20	15	2.2
2014	1.91	29	1.6
2013	1.48	18	1.8
2012	1.25	29	2.0
2011	0.97	47	1.8
2010	0.66	22	1.4
2009	0.54	10	1.7
2008	0.49	32	2.1
2007	0.37	23	1.2
2006	0.30	-	1.3
2005	0.30	-	1.5

PEPSICO INC.

PepsiCo, Inc. operates as a food and beverage company worldwide. Its Frito-Lay North America segment offers Lay's potato chips, Doritos tortilla chips, Cheetos cheese-flavored snacks, Tostitos tortilla chips, branded dips, Ruffles potato chips, Fritos corn chips, and Santitas tortilla chips.

Website: http://www.pepsico.com

RANKINGS; OVERALL; #55, WITHIN CONSUMER STAPLES; #11

Category	Value	Ranking
Dividend Yield	2.75	99
Dividend Growth	7.5	155
Trailing Price/Earnings	22.6	174
S&P Financial Rating	A++	40
Beta	0.70	50
Ranking Score		518

Date	Yearly Dividend	Dividend Growth %	Average Dividend Yield %
2015	2.79	10	2.9
2014	2.53	13	2.7
2013	2.24	5	2.7
2012	2.13	5	3.1
2011	2.03	7	3.1
2010	1.89	6	2.9
2009	1.78	8	2.9
2008	1.65	15	3.0
2007	1.43	23	1.9
2006	1.16	15	1.9
2005	1.01	19	1.7

ARCHERDANIELS MIDLAND COMPANY

Archer-Daniels-Midland Company procures, transports, stores, processes, and merchandises agricultural commodities and products. The company's Oilseeds Processing segment originates, merchandises, crushes, and processes soybeans and soft seeds into vegetable oils and protein meals.

Website: http://www.adm.com

RANKINGS; OVERALL; #56, WITHIN CONSUMER STAPLES; #12

Category	Value	Ranking
Dividend Yield	2.22	140
Dividend Growth	12.5	90
Trailing Price/Earnings	14	60
S&P Financial Rating	A+	80
Beta	1.1	150
Ranking Score		520

Date	Yearly Dividend	Dividend Growth %	Average Dividend Yield %
2015	1.12	17	2.4
2014	0.96	26	1.9
2013	0.76	9	1.8
2012	0.70	13	2.6
2011	0.62	7	2.3
2010	0.58	7	2.0
2009	0.54	10	1.8
2008	0.49	14	1.8
2007	0.43	16	1.0
2006	0.37	16	1.3
2005	0.32	7	1.4

EATON CORPORATION PLC

Eaton Corporation plc operates as a power management company worldwide. Its Electrical Products segment offers electrical components, industrial components, residential products, wiring devices, and structural support systems, as well as single phase power quality, emergency lighting, fire detection, circuit protection, and lighting products.

Website: http://www.eaton.com

RANKINGS; OVERALL; #57, WITHIN INDUSTRIALS; #6

Category	Value	Ranking
Dividend Yield	3.08	72
Dividend Growth	12	101
Trailing Price/Earnings	14.4	67
S&P Financial Rating	A+	80
Beta	1.3	200
Ranking Score		520

Date	Yearly Dividend	Dividend Growth %	Average Dividend Yield %
2015	2.20	12	3.5
2014	1.96	17	2.9
2013	1.68	11	2.2
2012	1.52	12	2.8
2011	1.36	26	3.1
2010	1.08	8	2.1
2009	1.00	-	3.1
2008	1.00	16	4.0
2007	0.86	16	1.8
2006	0.74	19	2.0
2005	0.62	15	1.9

NextEra Energy Inc.

NextEra Energy, Inc., through its subsidiaries, generates, transmits, and distributes electric energy in the United States and Canada. The company generates electricity from gas, oil, solar, coal, petroleum coke, nuclear, and wind sources.

Website: http://www.nexteraenergy.com

RANKINGS; OVERALL; #58, WITHIN UTILITIES; #5

Category	Value	Ranking
Dividend Yield	3.08	73
Dividend Growth	8	147
Trailing Price/Earnings	19.3	130
S&P Financial Rating	A	120
Beta	0.7	50
Ranking Score		520

Date	Yearly Dividend	Dividend Growth %	Average Dividend Yield %
2015	3.08	6	3.0
2014	2.90	10	2.7
2013	2.64	10	3.1
2012	2.40	9	3.5
2011	2.20	10	3.6
2010	2.00	6	3.9
2009	1.89	6	3.6
2008	1.78	9	3.5
2007	1.64	9	2.4
2006	1.50	6	2.8
2005	1.42	9	3.4

TEXAS INSTRUMENTS INC.

Texas Instruments Incorporated designs, manufactures, and sells semiconductors to electronics designers and manufacturers worldwide. It operates through two segments, Analog and Embedded Processing.

Website: http://www.ti.com

RANKINGS; OVERALL; #59, WITHIN TECHNOLOGY; #8

Category	Value	Ranking
Dividend Yield	2.52	116
Dividend Growth	21.5	41
Trailing Price/Earnings	22.7	176
S&P Financial Rating	A++	40
Beta	1.1	150
Ranking Score		**523**

Date	Yearly Dividend	Dividend Growth %	Average Dividend Yield %
2015	1.40	13	2.6
2014	1.24	16	2.3
2013	1.07	49	2.4
2012	0.72	29	2.3
2011	0.56	14	1.9
2010	0.49	9	1.5
2009	0.45	10	1.7
2008	0.41	37	2.6
2007	0.30	130	0.9
2006	0.13	18	0.5
2005	0.11	22	0.3

MAGNA INTERNATIONAL INC.

Magna International Inc. develops, manufactures, engineers, supplies, and sells automotive products. It operates through North America, Europe, Asia, and Rest of World segments.

Website: http://www.magna.com

RANKINGS; OVERALL; #60, WITHIN INDUSTRIALS; #7

Category	Value	Ranking
Dividend Yield	1.73	173
Dividend Growth	24.5	30
Trailing Price/Earnings	11.5	26
S&P Financial Rating	A	120
Beta	1.2	175
Ranking Score		524

Date	Yearly Dividend	Dividend Growth %	Average Dividend Yield %
2015	0.88	16	1.7
2014	0.76	19	1.4
2013	0.64	16	1.6
2012	0.55	10	2.2
2011	0.50	138	3.0
2010	0.21	320	0.8
2009	0.05	-84	0.7
2008	0.32	10	4.2
2007	0.29	-24	1.4
2006	0.38	-	1.9
2005	0.38	3	2.1

AETNA INC.

Aetna Inc. operates as a health care benefits company in the United States. It operates through three segments: Health Care, Group Insurance, and Large Case Pensions. The Health Care segment offers medical, pharmacy benefit management services, dental, behavioral health, and vision plans on an insured basis, and an employer-funded or administrative basis.

Website: http://www.aetna.com

RANKINGS; OVERALL; #61, WITHIN HEALTHCARE; #8

Category	Value	Ranking
Dividend Yield	0.93	231
Dividend Growth	78.5	3
Trailing Price/Earnings	14.9	71
S&P Financial Rating	A	120
Beta	0.90	100
Ranking Score		**528**

Date	Yearly Dividend	Dividend Growth %	Average Dividend Yield %
2015	1.00	11	0.9
2014	0.90	13	1.0
2013	0.80	14	1.2
2012	0.70	56	1.5
2011	0.45	1025	1.1
2010	0.04	-	0.1
2009	0.04	-	0.1
2008	0.04	-	0.1
2007	0.04	-	0.1
2006	0.04	-	0.1
2005	-	-	-

CAPITAL ONE FINANCIAL CORPORATION

Capital One Financial Corporation operates as the bank holding company for the Capital One Bank (USA), National Association (COBNA); and Capital One, National Association (CONA), which provide various financial products and services in the United States, the United Kingdom, and Canada.

Website: http://www.capitalone.com

RANKINGS; OVERALL; #62, WITHIN FINANCIAL; #8

Category	Value	Ranking
Dividend Yield	1.95	160
Dividend Growth	12.5	92
Trailing Price/Earnings	9.8	7
S&P Financial Rating	A	120
Beta	1.1	150
Ranking Score		529

Date	Yearly Dividend	Dividend Growth %	Average Dividend Yield %
2015	1.50	25	1.9
2014	1.20	26	1.5
2013	0.95	375	1.2
2012	0.20	-	0.4
2011	0.20	-	0.5
2010	0.20	-62	0.5
2009	0.53	-66	1.4
2008	1.50	1264	4.7
2007	0.11	-	0.2
2006	0.11	-	0.1
2005	0.11	-	0.1

ANTHEM INC.

Anthem.

Anthem, Inc., through its subsidiaries, operates as a health benefits company in the United States. It operates through three segments: Commercial and Specialty Business, Government Business, and Other. The company offers a spectrum of network-based managed care health benefit plans to large and small employer, individual, Medicaid, and senior markets.

Website: http://www.antheminc.com

RANKINGS; OVERALL; #63, WITHIN HEALTHCARE; #9

Category	Value	Ranking
Dividend Yield	1.62	181
Dividend Growth	20.6	44
Trailing Price/Earnings	16.3	90
S&P Financial Rating	A	120
Beta	0.90	100
Ranking Score		535

Date	Yearly Dividend	Dividend Growth %	Average Dividend Yield %
2015	2.50	43	1.7
2014	1.75	17	1.4
2013	1.50	30	1.6
2012	1.15	15	1.9
2011	1.00	-	1.5
2010	-	-	-
2009	-	-	-
2008	-	-	-
2007	-	-	-
2006	-	-	-
2005	-	-	-

CATERPILLAR INC.

Caterpillar Inc. manufactures and sells construction and mining equipment, diesel and natural gas engines, industrial gas turbines, and diesel-electric locomotives worldwide.

Website: http://www.caterpillar.com

RANKINGS; OVERALL; #64, WITHIN INDUSTRIALS; #8

Category	Value	Ranking
Dividend Yield	3.22	63
Dividend Growth	8	143
Trailing Price/Earnings	13.2	49
S&P Financial Rating	A+	80
Beta	1.3	200
Ranking Score		535

Date	Yearly Dividend	Dividend Growth %	Average Dividend Yield %
2015	3.01	16	3.8
2014	2.60	52	2.8
2013	1.72	-12	1.9
2012	1.96	9	2.2
2011	1.80	5	2.0
2010	1.72	2	1.8
2009	1.68	8	3.0
2008	1.56	18	3.5
2007	1.32	20	1.8
2006	1.10	21	1.8
2005	0.91	17	1.6

Infosys Limited, together with its subsidiaries, provides business consulting, technology, engineering, and outsourcing services in North America, Europe, India, and internationally.

Website: http://www.infosys.com

RANKINGS; OVERALL; #65, WITHIN TECHNOLOGY; #9

Category	Value	Ranking
Dividend Yield	1..91	166
Dividend Growth	12.5	94
Trailing Price/Earnings	19.7	136
S&P Financial Rating	A++	40
Beta	0.9	100
Ranking Score		**536**

Date	Yearly Dividend	Dividend Growth %	Average Dividend Yield %
2015	0.36	20	2.0
2014	0.30	43	1.9
2013	0.21	-8	1.4
2012	0.23	21	1.5
2011	0.19	-39	1.4
2010	0.31	158	0.7
2009	0.12	-45	0.8
2008	0.22	450	1.5
2007	0.04	-71	0.6
2006	0.14	250	0.9
2005	0.04	185	0.3

MEDTRONIC PLC.

Medtronic plc manufactures and sells device-based medical therapies worldwide.

Website: http://www.medtronic.com

RANKINGS; OVERALL; #66, WITHIN HEALTHCARE; #10

Category	Value	Ranking
Dividend Yield	1.63	180
Dividend Growth	15.5	66
Trailing Price/Earnings	19.1	129
S&P Financial Rating	A++	40
Beta	1.0	125
Ranking Score		540

Date	Yearly Dividend	Dividend Growth %	Average Dividend Yield %
2015	1.52	25	2.0
2014	1.22	9	1.7
2013	1.12	8	1.9
2012	1.04	7	2.5
2011	0.97	8	2.4
2010	0.90	10	2.3
2009	0.82	13	1.8
2008	0.75	50	2.2
2007	0.50	14	0.9
2006	0.44	13	0.8
2005	0.39	22	0.6

FORD

Ford Motor Company manufactures and distributes automobiles worldwide. The company operates through two sectors, Automotive and Financial Services. The Automotive sector develops, manufactures, distributes, and services vehicles, parts, and accessories.

Website: http://www.ford.com

RANKINGS; OVERALL; #67, WITHIN CONSUMER DISCRETIONARY; #3

Category	Value	Ranking
Dividend Yield	3.86	34
Dividend Growth	19	49
Trailing Price/Earnings	14	61
S&P Financial Rating	B+	200
Beta	1.3	200
Ranking Score		**544**

Date	Yearly Dividend	Dividend Growth %	Average Dividend Yield %
2015	0.60	20	4.0
2014	0.50	25	3.1
2013	0.40	100	2.6
2012	0.20	-	1.8
2011	-	-	-
2010	-	-	-
2009	-	-	-
2008	-	-	-
2007	-	-	-
2006	0.25	-38	3.2
2005	0.40	-	3.8

BECTON, DICKINSON AND COMPANY

Becton, Dickinson and Company develops, manufactures, and sells medical devices, instrument systems, and reagents worldwide.

Website: http://www.bd.com

RANKINGS; OVERALL; #68, WITHIN HEALTHCARE; #11

Category	Value	Ranking
Dividend Yield	1.69	176
Dividend Growth	12.5	91
Trailing Price/Earnings	22.1	165
S&P Financial Rating	A++	40
Beta	0.8	75
Ranking Score		**547**

Date	Yearly Dividend	Dividend Growth %	Average Dividend Yield %
2015	2.40	10	1.7
2014	2.18	10	1.9
2013	1.98	10	2.2
2012	1.80	10	2.4
2011	1.64	11	2.0
2010	1.48	12	2.0
2009	1.32	15	1.9
2008	1.14	16	1.3
2007	0.98	14	1.3
2006	0.86	19	1.4
2005	0.72	20	1.3

STRYKER CORPORATION

stryker®

Stryker Corporation, together with its subsidiaries, operates as a medical technology company. The company operates through three segments: Orthopaedics, MedSurg, and Neurotechnology and Spine.

Website: http://www.strykercorp.com

RANKINGS; OVERALL; #69, WITHIN HEALTHCARE; #12

Category	Value	Ranking
Dividend Yield	1.49	190
Dividend Growth	23.5	32
Trailing Price/Earnings	24.2	188
S&P Financial Rating	A++	40
Beta	0.90	100
Ranking Score		550

Date	Yearly Dividend	Dividend Growth %	Average Dividend Yield %
2015	1.42	13	1.5
2014	1.26	15	1.3
2013	1.10	22	1.5
2012	0.90	20	1.7
2011	0.75	19	1.5
2010	0.63	320	1.2
2009	0.15	-63	1.1
2008	0.40	21	1.0
2007	0.33	50	0.4
2006	0.22	100	0.4
2005	0.11	22	0.3

AMERICAN EXPRESS COMPANY

American Express Company, together with its subsidiaries, provides charge and credit payment card products and travel-related services to consumers and businesses worldwide.

Website: http://www.americanexpress.com

RANKINGS; OVERALL; #70, WITHIN FINANCIAL; #9

Category	Value	Ranking
Dividend Yield	1.34	199
Dividend Growth	13	87
Trailing Price/Earnings	15.1	77
S&P Financial Rating	A++	40
Beta	1.1	150
Ranking Score		553

Date	Yearly Dividend	Dividend Growth %	Average Dividend Yield %
2015	1.10	-	1.4
2014	1.10	-11	1.4
2013	1.24	88	1.0
2012	0.66	-17.5	1.4
2011	0.80	11	1.5
2010	0.72	-	1.7
2009	0.72	-	1.8
2008	0.72	14	3.9
2007	0.63	11	1.2
2006	0.57	19	0.9
2005	0.48	33	0.9

COLGATEPALMOLIVE CO.

Colgate-Palmolive Company, together with its subsidiaries, manufactures and markets consumer products worldwide. It operates in two segments: Oral, Personal and Home Care; and Pet Nutrition.

Website: http://www.colgatepalmolive.com

RANKINGS; OVERALL; #71, WITHIN CONSUMER STAPLES; #13

Category	Value	Ranking
Dividend Yield	2.26	135
Dividend Growth	11	111
Trailing Price/Earnings	29	220
S&P Financial Rating	A++	40
Beta	0.7	50
Ranking Score		**556**

Date	Yearly Dividend	Dividend Growth %	Average Dividend Yield %
2015	1.50	6	2.2
2014	1.42	7	2.1
2013	1.33	9	2.0
2012	1.22	7	2.3
2011	1.14	12	2.5
2010	1.02	20	2.5
2009	0.86	10	2.1
2008	0.78	11	2.3
2007	0.70	11	1.8
2006	0.63	13	1.9
2005	0.56	17	2.0

UNITED TECHNOLOGIES CORPORATION

United Technologies Corporation provides technology products and services to building systems and aerospace industries worldwide.

Website: http://www.utc.com

RANKINGS; OVERALL; #72, WITHIN INDUSTRIALS; #9

Category	Value	Ranking
Dividend Yield	2.23	139
Dividend Growth	10	126
Trailing Price/Earnings	17.2	104
S&P Financial Rating	A++	40
Beta	1.1	150
Ranking Score		**559**

Date	Yearly Dividend	Dividend Growth %	Average Dividend Yield %
2015	2.56	8	2.4
2014	2.36	7	2.1
2013	2.20	8	1.9
2012	2.03	9	2.5
2011	1.87	10	2.6
2010	1.70	10	2.2
2009	1.54	14	2.2
2008	1.35	15	2.5
2007	1.17	15	1.5
2006	1.02	16	1.6
2005	0.88	26	1.6

NORFOLK SOUTHERN CORPORATION –

Norfolk Southern Corporation, together with its subsidiaries, engages in the rail transportation of raw materials, intermediate products, and finished goods.

Website: http://www.nscorp.com

RANKINGS; OVERALL; #73, WITHIN INDUSTRIALS; #10

Category	Value	Ranking
Dividend Yield	2.35	124
Dividend Growth	12	102
Trailing Price/Earnings	17.3	105
S&P Financial Rating	A+	80
Beta	1.1	150
Ranking Score		561

Date	Yearly Dividend	Dividend Growth %	Average Dividend Yield %
2015	2.36	6	2.6
2014	2.22	9	2.0
2013	2.04	11	2.2
2012	1.94	17	3.1
2011	1.66	19	2.3
2010	1.40	3	2.2
2009	1.36	11	2.6
2008	1.22	27	2.6
2007	0.96	41	1.9
2006	0.68	42	1.4
2005	0.48	33	1.1

BLACKROCK, INC.

BLACKROCK®

BlackRock, Inc. is a publicly owned investment manager. The firm primarily provides its services to institutional, intermediary, and individual investors. It also manages accounts for corporate, public, union and industry pension plans, insurance companies, third-party mutual funds, endowments, foundations, charities, corporations, official institutions, and banks.55 East 52nd Street

Website: http://www.blackrock.com

RANKINGS; OVERALL; #74, WITHIN FINANCIAL; #10

Category	Value	Ranking
Dividend Yield	2.38	122
Dividend Growth	23	34
Trailing Price/Earnings	18.3	116
S&P Financial Rating	A	120
Beta	1.2	175
Ranking Score		**567**

Date	Yearly Dividend	Dividend Growth %	Average Dividend Yield %
2015	8.72	13	2.5
2014	7.72	15	2.2
2013	6.72	12	2.1
2012	6.00	0.3	2.9
2011	5.98	50	2.6
2010	4.00	28	2.1
2009	3.12	-	1.3
2008	3.12	16	2.3
2007	2.68	60	1.2
2006	1.68	40	1.1
2005	1.20	20	1.1

COMCAST CORPORATION

Comcast Corporation operates as a media and technology company worldwide. It operates through Cable Communications, Cable Networks, Broadcast Television, Filmed Entertainment, and Theme Parks segments.

Website: http://www.comcast.com

RANKINGS; OVERALL; #75, WITHIN FINANCIAL; #11

Category	Value	Ranking
Dividend Yield	1.72	172
Dividend Growth	49.5	10
Trailing Price/Earnings	20	140
S&P Financial Rating	A	120
Beta	1.0	125
Ranking Score		567

Date	Yearly Dividend	Dividend Growth %	Average Dividend Yield %
2015	1.00	12	1.7
2014	0.90	15	1.5
2013	0.78	20	1.5
2012	0.65	44	1.7
2011	0.45	18	1.9
2010	0.38	27	1.7
2009	0.30	20	1.6
2008	0.25	-	1.1
2007	-	-	-
2006	-	-	-
2005	-	-	-

CVS HEALTH CORPORATION

CVS Health Corporation, together with its subsidiaries, provides integrated pharmacy health care services in the United States. The company operates through Pharmacy Services and Retail Pharmacy segments.

Website: http://www.cvshealth.com

RANKINGS; OVERALL; #76, WITHIN HEALTHCARE; #13

Category	Value	Ranking
Dividend Yield	1.42	192
Dividend Growth	26	24
Trailing Price/Earnings	22.5	172
S&P Financial Rating	A+	80
Beta	0.9	100
Ranking Score		568

Date	Yearly Dividend	Dividend Growth %	Average Dividend Yield %
2015	1.40	27	1.4
2014	1.10	22	1.1
2013	0.90	38	1.3
2012	0.65	30	1.3
2011	0.50	43	1.2
2010	0.35	13	1.0
2009	0.31	19	1.0
2008	0.26	13	0.9
2007	0.23	44	0.6
2006	0.16	7	0.5
2005	0.15	15	0.6

VALERO ENERGY CORPORATION

Valero Energy Corporation operates as an independent petroleum refining and marketing company in the United States, Canada, the Caribbean, the United Kingdom, and Ireland.

Website: http://www.valero.com

RANKINGS; OVERALL; #77, WITHIN ENERGY; #7

Category	Value	Ranking
Dividend Yield	2.76	98
Dividend Growth	6	168
Trailing Price/Earnings	8.8	3
S&P Financial Rating	A+	80
Beta	1.4	225
Ranking Score		574

Date	Yearly Dividend	Dividend Growth %	Average Dividend Yield %
2015	1.70	62	2.8
2014	1.05	24	2.1
2013	0.85	31	1.7
2012	0.65	116	1.9
2011	0.30	50	1.4
2010	0.20	-66	0.9
2009	0.60	5	3.6
2008	0.57	19	2.6
2007	0.48	60	0.7
2006	0.30	58	0.6
2005	0.19	46	0.4

SEMPRA ENERGY

Sempra Energy operates as an energy services holding company worldwide. The company's San Diego Gas & Electric Company segment transmits and distributes electricity and/or natural gas.

Website: http://www.sempra.com

RANKINGS; OVERALL; #78, WITHIN UTILITIES; #6

Category	Value	Ranking
Dividend Yield	2.68	104
Dividend Growth	12.5	100
Trailing Price/Earnings	23.1	177
S&P Financial Rating	A	120
Beta	0.8	75
Ranking Score		576

Date	Yearly Dividend	Dividend Growth %	Average Dividend Yield %
2015	2.80	6	2.7
2014	2.64	5	2.4
2013	2.52	5	2.8
2012	2.40	25	3.4
2011	1.92	23	3.5
2010	1.56	-	3.0
2009	1.56	14	2.8
2008	1.37	10	3.2
2007	1.24	3	2.0
2006	1.20	3	2.1
2005	1.16	16	2.6

Cardinal Health, Inc. operates as a healthcare services and products company worldwide. The company operates in two segments, Pharmaceutical and Medical.

Website: http://www.cardinalhealth.com

RANKINGS; OVERALL; #79, WITHIN HEALTHCARE; #14

Category	Value	Ranking
Dividend Yield	1.62	182
Dividend Growth	17.5	54
Trailing Price/Earnings	26.3	201
S&P Financial Rating	A++	40
Beta	0.9	100
Ranking Score		577

Date	Yearly Dividend	Dividend Growth %	Average Dividend Yield %
2015	1.41	13	1.7
2014	1.25	15	2.0
2013	1.09	24	2.5
2012	0.88	7	2.1
2011	0.82	11	2.1
2010	0.74	23	2.3
2009	0.60	15	1.5
2008	0.52	44	0.9
2007	0.36	-	0.5
2006	0.36	140	0.5
2005	0.15	25	0.3

VIACOM, INC.

Viacom Inc. operates as an entertainment content company in the United States and internationally. The company creates television programs, motion pictures, short-form video, applications, games, consumer products, social media, and other entertainment content. It operates in two segments, Media Networks and Filmed Entertainment.

Website: http://www.viacom.com

RANKINGS; OVERALL; #80, WITHIN CONSUMER DISCRETIONARY; #4

Category	Value	Ranking
Dividend Yield	1.92	164
Dividend Growth	16.4	59
Trailing Price/Earnings	13	45
S&P Financial Rating	B++	160
Beta	1.1	150
Ranking Score		578

Date	Yearly Dividend	Dividend Growth %	Average Dividend Yield %
2015	1.46	16	2.3
2014	1.26	10	1.5
2013	1.15	10	1.8
2012	1.05	31	2.3
2011	0.80	166	1.8
2010	0.30	-	0.90
2009	-	-	-
2008	-	-	-
2007	-	-	-
2006	-	-	-
2005	-	-	-

SYSCO CORPORATION

Viacom Inc. operates as an entertainment content company in the United States and internationally. The company creates television programs, motion pictures, short-form video, applications, games, consumer products, social media, and other entertainment content. It operates in two segments, Media Networks and Filmed Entertainment.

Website: http://www.sysco.com

RANKINGS; OVERALL; #81, WITHIN CONSUMER STAPLES; #14

Category	Value	Ranking
Dividend Yield	3.32	54
Dividend Growth	5.5	174
Trailing Price/Earnings	25.5	197
S&P Financial Rating	A+	80
Beta	0.8	75
Ranking Score		580

Date	Yearly Dividend	Dividend Growth %	Average Dividend Yield %
2015	1.19	3	3.1
2014	1.16	5	3.3
2013	1.11	4	3.5
2012	1.07	4	3.7
2011	1.03	4	3.5
2010	0.99	5	3.6
2009	0.94	11	3.7
2008	0.85	15	2.7
2007	0.74	12	2.2
2006	0.66	18	2.1
2005	0.56	17	1.6

SUNCOR ENERGY INC.

Suncor Energy Inc. operates as an integrated energy company. The company primarily focuses on developing petroleum resource basins in Canada's Athabasca oil sands.

Website: http://www.suncor.com

RANKINGS; OVERALL; #82, WITHIN BASIC MATERIAL; #4

Category	Value	Ranking
Dividend Yield	2.92	85
Dividend Growth	25	27
Trailing Price/Earnings	21	151
S&P Financial Rating	A	120
Beta	1.3	200
Ranking Score		583

Date	Yearly Dividend	Dividend Growth %	Average Dividend Yield %
2015	1.14	12	3.1
2014	1.02	34	2.9
2013	0.76	52	2.0
2012	0.50	16	1.5
2011	0.43	8	1.5
2010	0.40	33	1.0
2009	0.30	50	0.8
2008	0.20	5	1.0
2007	0.19	27	0.3
2006	0.15	25	0.3
2005	0.12	9	0.3

AMERIPRISE FINANCIAL INC.

Ameriprise Financial, Inc., through its subsidiaries, provides various financial products and services to individual and institutional clients in the United States and internationally.

Website: http://www.ameriprise.com

RANKINGS; OVERALL; #83, WITHIN FINANCIAL; #12

Category	Value	Ranking
Dividend Yield	2.15	147
Dividend Growth	21.5	36
Trailing Price/Earnings	15.9	86
S&P Financial Rating	A	120
Beta	1.3	200
Ranking Score		589

Date	Yearly Dividend	Dividend Growth %	Average Dividend Yield %
2015	2.59	15	2.1
2014	2.26	12	1.7
2013	2.01	41	1.8
2012	1.43	64	2.3
2011	0.87	23	1.8
2010	0.71	4	1.2
2009	0.68	6	1.8
2008	0.64	14	2.7
2007	0.56	27	1.0
2006	0.44	300	0.8
2005	0.11	-	0.3

THE BOEING COMPANY

The Boeing Company, together with its subsidiaries, designs, develops, manufactures, sells, services, and supports commercial jetliners, military aircraft, satellites, missile defense, human space flight, and launch systems and services worldwide.

Website: http://www.boeing.com

RANKINGS; OVERALL; #84, WITHIN INDUSTRIALS; #11

Category	Value	Ranking
Dividend Yield	2.81	90
Dividend Growth	7	159
Trailing Price/Earnings	21	150
S&P Financial Rating	A++	40
Beta	1.1	150
Ranking Score		589

Date	Yearly Dividend	Dividend Growth %	Average Dividend Yield %
2015	3.64	25	2.5
2014	2.92	51	2.3
2013	1.94	10	1.4
2012	1.76	5	2.3
2011	1.68	-	2.3
2010	1.68	-	2.6
2009	1.68	5	3.1
2008	1.60	14	3.8
2007	1.40	17	1.6
2006	1.20	20	1.4
2005	1.00	30	1.4

PFIZER INC.

Pfizer Inc., a biopharmaceutical company, discovers, develops, manufactures, and sells healthcare products worldwide. The company operates through Global Innovative Pharmaceutical (GIP); Global Vaccines, Oncology and Consumer Healthcare (VOC); and Global Established Pharmaceutical (GEP) segments

Website: http://www.pfizer.com

RANKINGS; OVERALL; #85, WITHIN HEALTHCARE; #15

Category	Value	Ranking
Dividend Yield	3.28	57
Dividend Growth	-5	229
Trailing Price/Earnings	24.6	191
S&P Financial Rating	A++	40
Beta	0.8	75
Ranking Score		592

Date	Yearly Dividend	Dividend Growth %	Average Dividend Yield %
2015	1.12	8	3.3
2014	1.04	8	3.3
2013	0.96	9	3.1
2012	0.88	10	3.5
2011	0.80	11	3.7
2010	0.72	-10	4.1
2009	0.80	-37.5	4.4
2008	1.28	10	7.2
2007	1.16	21	5.1
2006	0.96	26	3.7
2005	0.76	12	3.3

T. ROWE PRICE GROUP, INC.

T. Rowe Price Group, Inc. is a publicly owned asset management holding company. The firm provides its services to individuals, institutional investors, retirement plans, financial intermediaries, and institutions.

Website: http://www.troweprice.com

RANKINGS; OVERALL; #86, WITHIN FINANCIAL; #13

Category	Value	Ranking
Dividend Yield	2.56	112
Dividend Growth	11	115
Trailing Price/Earnings	17.9	111
S&P Financial Rating	A+	80
Beta	1.2	175
Ranking Score		**593**

Date	Yearly Dividend	Dividend Growth %	Average Dividend Yield %
2015	2.08	18	2.7
2014	1.76	16	2.1
2013	1.52	12	1.8
2012	1.36	10	2.1
2011	1.24	15	2.2
2010	1.08	8	1.7
2009	1.00	4	1.9
2008	0.96	28	2.7
2007	0.75	27	1.2
2006	0.59	20	1.4
2005	0.49	22.5	1.4

CORNING INC.

CORNING

Corning Incorporated manufactures and sells specialty glasses, ceramics, and related materials worldwide. The company operates through five segments: Display Technologies, Optical Communications, Environmental Technologies, Specialty Materials, and Life Sciences.

Website: http://www.corning.com

RANKINGS; OVERALL; #87, WITHIN INDUSTRIALS; #12

Category	Value	Ranking
Dividend Yield	2.31	128
Dividend Growth	19.5	48
Trailing Price/Earnings	13.5	57
S&P Financial Rating	B++	160
Beta	1.3	200
Ranking Score		593

Date	Yearly Dividend	Dividend Growth %	Average Dividend Yield %
2015	0.36	-30	1.8
2014	0.52	33	1.7
2013	0.39	22	2.2
2012	0.32	39	2.5
2011	0.23	15	1.7
2010	0.20	-	1.0
2009	0.20	-	1.0
2008	0.20	100	2.1
2007	0.10	-	0.4
2006	-	-	-
2005	-	-	-

DOMINION RESOURCES INC.

Dominion Resources, Inc. produces and transports energy in the United States. The company operates through three segments: Dominion Virginia Power (DVP), Dominion Generation, and Dominion Energy.

Website: http://www.dom.com

RANKINGS; OVERALL; #88, WITHIN UTILITIES; #7

Category	Value	Ranking
Dividend Yield	3.66	42
Dividend Growth	7.5	150
Trailing Price/Earnings	25.2	193
S&P Financial Rating	B++	160
Beta	0.7	50
Ranking Score		595

Date	Yearly Dividend	Dividend Growth %	Average Dividend Yield %
2015	2.59	8	3.7
2014	2.40	7	3.1
2013	2.25	7	3.5
2012	2.11	7	4.1
2011	1.97	8	3.7
2010	1.83	5	4.3
2009	1.75	11	4.5
2008	1.58	8	4.4
2007	1.46	6	3.1
2006	1.38	3	3.3
2005	1.34	3	3.5

AUTOMATIC DATA PROCESSING INC.

Automatic Data Processing, Inc., together with its subsidiaries, provides business process outsourcing services worldwide. The company operates through two segments, Employer Services and Professional Employer Organization (PEO) Services.

Website: http://www.adp.com

RANKINGS; OVERALL; #89, WITHIN TECHNOLOGY; #10

Category	Value	Ranking
Dividend Yield	2.29	130
Dividend Growth	10.5	117
Trailing Price/Earnings	27.8	211
S&P Financial Rating	A++	40
Beta	0.9	100
Ranking Score		**598**

Date	Yearly Dividend	Dividend Growth %	Average Dividend Yield %
2015	1.95	4	
2014	1.88	11	2.3
2013	1.70	10	2.2
2012	1.55	9	2.9
2011	1.42	6	2.7
2010	1.34	8	3.0
2009	1.24	19	3.1
2008	1.04	25	3.1
2007	0.83	22	2.2
2006	0.68	7	1.6
2005	0.61	7	1.4

HONEYWELL INTERNATIONAL INC.

Honeywell

Honeywell International Inc. operates as a diversified technology and manufacturing company worldwide.

Website: http://www.honeywell.com

RANKINGS; OVERALL; #90, WITHIN INDUSTRIALS; #13

Category	Value	Ranking
Dividend Yield	2.04	154
Dividend Growth	9	132
Trailing Price/Earnings	18.7	122
S&P Financial Rating	A++	40
Beta	1.1	150
Ranking Score		598

Date	Yearly Dividend	Dividend Growth %	Average Dividend Yield %
2015	2.15	15	2.1
2014	1.87	11	1.9
2013	1.68	10	1.8
2012	1.53	12	2.4
2011	1.37	13	2.5
2010	1.21	-	2.3
2009	1.21	10	3.1
2008	1.10	10	3.4
2007	1.00	10	1.6
2006	0.91	10	2.0
2005	0.83	11	2.2

METLIFE INC.

MetLife

MetLife, Inc. provides life insurance, annuities, employee benefits, and asset management products in the United States, Japan, Latin America, Asia, Europe, and the Middle East.

Website: http://www.metlife.com

RANKINGS; OVERALL; #91, WITHIN FINANCIAL; #14

Category	Value	Ranking
Dividend Yield	2.88	89
Dividend Growth	7	162
Trailing Price/Earnings	8.9	4
S&P Financial Rating	A	120
Beta	1.4	225
Ranking Score		**600**

Date	Yearly Dividend	Dividend Growth %	Average Dividend Yield %
2015	1.48	11	2.9
2014	1.33	32	2.5
2013	1.01	36	1.9
2012	0.74	-	2.3
2011	0.74	-	2.4
2010	0.74	-	1.7
2009	0.74	-	2.1
2008	0.74	-	2.1
2007	0.74	25	1.2
2006	0.59	13	1.0
2005	0.52	13	1.1

VENTAS INC.

Ventas, Inc. is a publicly owned real estate investment trust. The firm engages in investment, management, financing, and leasing of properties in the health-care industry.

Website: http://www.ventasreit.com

RANKINGS; OVERALL; #92, WITHIN REAL ESTATE INVESTMENT; #2

Category	Value	Ranking
Dividend Yield	4.67	15
Dividend Growth	7.7	148
Trailing Price/Earnings	46	241
S&P Financial Rating	B+	200
Beta	0.8	75
Ranking Score		679

Date	Yearly Dividend	Dividend Growth %	Average Dividend Yield %
2015	3.04	2	4.7
2014	2.97	8	4.1
2013	2.74	10	4.8
2012	2.48	8	3.8
2011	2.30	7	3.1
2010	2.14	4	4.1
2009	2.05	-	4.7
2008	2.05	8	6.1
2007	1.90	20	4.2
2006	1.58	10	3.7
2005	1.44	11	4.5

WELLS FARGO & COMPANY

Wells Fargo & Company provides retail, commercial, and corporate banking services to individuals, businesses, and institutions.

Website: http://www.wellsfargo.com

RANKINGS; OVERALL; #93, WITHIN FINANCIAL; #15

Category	Value	Ranking
Dividend Yield	2.69	103
Dividend Growth	6.0	170
Trailing Price/Earnings	13	46
S&P Financial Rating	A	120
Beta	1.2	175
Ranking Score		679

Date	Yearly Dividend	Dividend Growth %	Average Dividend Yield %
2015	1.48	10	2.7
2014	1.35	17	2.7
2013	1.15	47	2.5
2012	0.78	90	2.5
2011	0.41	105	2.3
2010	0.20	-60	1.5
2009	0.49	-62	0.7
2008	1.30	10	1.8
2007	1.18	9	4.4
2006	1.08	8	3.9
2005	1.00	8	3.0

3M COMPANY

3M Science.
Applied to Life.™

3M Company operates as a diversified technology company worldwide.

Website: http://www.3m.com

RANKINGS; OVERALL; #94, WITHIN INDUSTRIALS; #14

Category	Value	Ranking
Dividend Yield	2.60	111
Dividend Growth	4.5	185
Trailing Price/Earnings	22.2	168
S&P Financial Rating	A++	40
Beta	1	125
Ranking Score		

Date	Yearly Dividend	Dividend Growth %	Average Dividend Yield %
2015	4.10	20	2.6
2014	3.42	35	2.7
2013	2.54	8	2.1
2012	2.36	7	1.8
2011	2.20	5	2.5
2010	2.10	3	2.7
2009	2.04	2	2.4
2008	2.00	4	2.5
2007	1.92	4	3.5
2006	1.84	10	2.3
2005	1.68	19	2.4

UNITED PARCEL SERVICE, INC.

United Parcel Service, Inc., a package delivery company, provides transportation, logistics, and financial services in the United States and internationally. It operates in three segments: U.S. Domestic Package, International Package, and Supply Chain & Freight.

Website: http://www.ups.com

RANKINGS; OVERALL; #95, WITHIN CONSUMER DISCRETIONARY; #5

Category	Value	Ranking
Dividend Yield	2.92	86
Dividend Growth	7	164
Trailing Price/Earnings	21.5	160
S&P Financial Rating	A	120
Beta	0.90	100
Ranking Score		630

Date	Yearly Dividend	Dividend Growth %	Average Dividend Yield %
2015	2.92	9	2.9
2014	2.68	8	3.0
2013	2.48	9	2.4
2012	2.28	10	2.4
2011	2.08	11	3.1
2010	1.88	4	2.8
2009	1.80	-	2.6
2008	1.80	7	3.1
2007	1.68	11	3.3
2006	1.52	15	2.4
2005	1.32	18	2.0

DIAGEO PLC

DIAGEO

Diageo plc produces, markets, and sells alcoholic beverages worldwide. It offers scotch and Irish whiskey, gin, vodka, rum, beer and spirits, Irish cream liqueurs, wine, Raki, tequila, Canadian and American whiskey, Cachaça, and brandy, as well as adult beverages and ready to drink products.

Website: http://www.diageo.com

RANKINGS; OVERALL; #96, WITHIN CONSUMER DISCRETIONARY; #6

Category	Value	Ranking
Dividend Yield	3.05	75
Dividend Growth	3.5	189
Trailing Price/Earnings	24.2	187
S&P Financial Rating	A+	80
Beta	0.90	100
Ranking Score		631

Date	Yearly Dividend	Dividend Growth %	Average Dividend Yield %
2015	3.46	3	3.0
2014	3.37	12	2.7
2013	2.99	8	2.6
2012	2.77	7	3.1
2011	2.60	14	3.5
2010	2.28	-4	3.5
2009	2.37	-13	4.1
2008	2.73	4	3.3
2007	2.63	-	3.4
2006	-	-	-
2005	-	-	-

J.P. Morgan Chase & Co.

JPMorgan Chase & Co.

JPMorgan Chase & Co. is a financial services firm. It operates through four segments: Consumer & Community Banking, Corporate & Investment Bank, Commercial Banking & Asset Management.

Website: http://www.jpmorganchase.com

RANKINGS; OVERALL; #97, WITHIN FINANCIAL; #16

Category	Value	Ranking
Dividend Yield	2.73	100
Dividend Growth	-3.5	228
Trailing Price/Earnings	10.7	17
S&P Financial Rating	A	120
Beta	1.2	175
Ranking Score		**640**

Date	Yearly Dividend	Dividend Growth %	Average Dividend Yield %
2015	1.72	9	2.7
2014	1.58	10	2.5
2013	1.44	20	2.5
2012	1.20	20	2.3
2011	1.00	400	2.6
2010	0.20	-	2.4
2009	0.20	-87	0.5
2008	1.52	3	1.3
2007	1.48	9	4.8
2006	1.36	-	3.3
2005	1.36	-	2.8

MAXIM INTEGRATED PRODUCTS, INC.

Maxim Integrated Products, Inc. designs, develops, manufactures, and markets various linear and mixed-signal integrated circuits worldwide. The company also provides a range of high-frequency process technologies and capabilities for use in custom designs.

Website: http://www.maximintegrated.com

RANKINGS; OVERALL; #98, WITHIN TECHNOLOGY; #11

Category	Value	Ranking
Dividend Yield	3.45	52
Dividend Growth	6.0	171
Trailing Price/Earnings	56.6	244
S&P Financial Rating	B++	160
Beta	1.0	125
Ranking Score		752

Date	Yearly Dividend	Dividend Growth %	Average Dividend Yield %
2015	1.12	8	3.5
2014	1.04	8	3.4
2013	0.96	8	3.3
2012	0.88	14	3.4
2011	0.84	5	3.7
2010	0.80	-	4.3
2009	0.80	7	5.3
2008	0.75	21	3.1
2007	0.62	30	2.0
2006	0.48	12	1.2
2005	0.38	26	0.9

KEYCORP.

KeyCorp operates as the bank holding company for KeyBank National Association that provides various retail and commercial banking services to individual, corporate, and institutional clients in the United States.

Website: http://www.key.com

RANKINGS; OVERALL; #99, WITHIN FINANCIAL; #17

Category	Value	Ranking
Dividend Yield	2.75	100
Dividend Growth	-24	247
Trailing Price/Earnings	10.4	15
S&P Financial Rating	B	240
Beta	1.15	150
Ranking Score		752

Date	Yearly Dividend	Dividend Growth %	Average Dividend Yield %
2015	0.29	16	2.1
2014	0.25	14	1.8
2013	0.22	22	1.6
2012	0.18	80	2.1
2011	0.10	150	1.3
2010	0.04	-55	0.5
2009	0.09	-91	1.7
2008	1.00	-32	11.7
2007	1.46	6	6.2
2006	1.38	6	3.6
2005	1.30	5	3.4

APPLE INC.

Apple Inc. designs, manufactures, and markets mobile communication and media devices, personal computers, and portable digital music players to consumers, small and mid-sized businesses, education, and enterprise and government customers worldwide.

Website: http://www.apple.com

RANKINGS; OVERALL; #100, WITHIN TECHNOLOGY; #12

Category	Value	Ranking
Dividend Yield	1.65	179
Dividend Growth	-39	348
Trailing Price/Earnings	17	101
S&P Financial Rating	A++	40
Beta	.90	100
Ranking Score		**768**

Date	Yearly Dividend	Dividend Growth %	Average Dividend Yield %
2015	1.98	9	1.7
2014	1.81	11	2.2
2013	1.63	329	2.3
2012	0.38	-	0.5
2011	-	-	-
2010	-	-	-
2009	-	-	-
2008	-	-	-
2007	-	-	-
2006	-	-	-
2005	-	-	-

CPSIA information can be obtained at www.ICGtesting.com
Printed in the USA
LVOW07*0250051016

507462LV00006B/36/P